UCAM-FOM Doctoral School of Business

Band 3

Clemens C. Jäger, Gonzalo Wandosell (Hrsg.)

**Yearbook 2016
UCAM-FOM Doctoral School of Business**

Shaker Verlag
Aachen 2016

Bibliografische Information der Deutschen Nationalbibliothek
Die Deutsche Nationalbibliothek verzeichnet diese Publikation in der Deutschen Nationalbibliografie; detaillierte bibliografische Daten sind im Internet über http://dnb.d-nb.de abrufbar.

Herausgebende Institution ist die FOM Hochschule für Oekonomie & Management gemeinnützige Gesellschaft mbH

Copyright Shaker Verlag 2016
Alle Rechte, auch das des auszugsweisen Nachdruckes, der auszugsweisen oder vollständigen Wiedergabe, der Speicherung in Datenverarbeitungs- anlagen und der Übersetzung, vorbehalten.

Printed in Germany.

ISBN 978-3-8440-4813-1
ISSN 2364-2955

Shaker Verlag GmbH • Postfach 101818 • 52018 Aachen
Telefon: 02407 / 95 96 - 0 • Telefax: 02407 / 95 96 - 9
Internet: www.shaker.de • E-Mail: info@shaker.de

PREFACE BY THE EDITOR

The long-standing cooperation between UCAM Universidad Católica San Antonio de Murcia and FOM University of Applied Sciences led to the introduction of a joint doctoral programme in 2010. This transnational PhD programme allows students from all over Europe to complete a doctoral degree in English at UCAM. The programme is consequently characterised by a high level of plurality and intensive cooperation between the universities, professors and doctoral candidates. The programme therefore follows the fundamental idea of European integration, bringing together different cultures beyond national borders.

The programme is also characterised by high quality standards and the intensive supervision of doctoral students. The participating universities believe that only a combination of academic excellence and intensive support services can produce outstanding academic results.

This publication series contains the first publications of the doctoral students in their academic careers and has been supported in the form of a critical discourse by professors of both UCAM and the FOM University of Applied Sciences.

Essen, October 2016

Prof. Dr. Dr. habil. Clemens C. Jäger
Dean of business of the FOM
University of Applied Sciences

Prof. Dr. Gonzalo Wandosell
Director of the UCAM - FOM Doctoral
School of Business

Prefacio

Después de un largo periodo de cooperación entre la Universidad Católica San Antonio de Murcia (UCAM) y la Universidad FOM, en el año 2010 se decidió poner en marcha un programa de doctorado con la participación conjunta de profesores de ambas instituciones. Gracias a este programa de doctorado transnacional estudiantes de toda Europa podrán realizar su doctorado en la UCAM en inglés. Este programa se caracteriza por una gran pluralidad y un intercambio intensivo entre las dos universidades, sus profesores y los doctorandos. Con ello, se unen las diferentes culturas nacionales, traspasando fronteras, y se pone en práctica la idea europea.

Otras importantes ventajas de este programa son la alta calidad a la que aspira y la tutela intensiva de los doctorandos. Las dos universidades que participan en él están convencidas de que sólo combinando la excelencia académica y una oferta de tutela intensiva, se pueden alcanzar resultados científicos extraordinarios.

La presente recopilación de artículos es el primer resultado del trabajo de los doctorandos, en su trayectoria investigadora, que ha sido supervisado, por profesores de ambas instituciones, con un debate crítico y riguroso.

Essen, Octubre 2016

Prof. Dr. Dr. habil. Clemens C. Jäger
Dean of business of the FOM
University of Applied Sciences

Prof. Dr. Gonzalo Wandosell
Director of the UCAM - FOM Doctoral
School of Business

Vorwort

Die langjährige Kooperation zwischen der UCAM Universidad Católica San Antonio de Murcia und der FOM Hochschule hat im Jahr 2010 zu einem gemeinsamen Promotionsprogramm geführt. Durch dieses grenzüberschreitende Promotionsprogramm wird es Studenten aus ganz Europa ermöglicht, an der UCAM in englischer Sprache zu promovieren. Das Programm zeichnet sich auch deshalb durch eine hohe Pluralität und ein intensives Miteinander zwischen den Hochschulen, Professoren und Doktoranden aus. Damit folgt dieses Programm dem europäischen Grundgedanken und führt die unterschiedlichen Kulturen länderübergreifend zusammen.

Das Programm zeichnet sich darüber hinaus durch einen hohen Qualitätsanspruch und durch eine enge Betreuung der Doktoranden aus. Denn nur die Kombination aus akademischer Exzellenz und einem intensiven Betreuungsangebot wird -nach der Überzeugung der beteiligten Hochschulen- zu hervorragenden wissenschaftlichen Ergebnissen führen.

Die vorliegende Publikationsreihe ist ein erstes öffentliches Ergebnis der Doktoranden auf ihrem akademischen Weg und wurde sowohl von Professoren der UCAM als auch der FOM Hochschule im Sinne eines kritischen Diskurses begleitet.

Essen, im Oktober 2016

Prof. Dr. Dr. habil. Clemens C. Jäger
Dekan für BWL an der FOM
Hochschule für Oekonomie & Management

Prof. Dr. Gonzalo Wandosell
Direktor an der UCAM-FOM Doctoral
School of Business

Bei Fragen zum Promotionsprogramm wenden Sie sich bitte an die zentrale Studienberatung unter der kostenlosen Nummer 0800 1959595 oder der Mailadresse studienberatung@fom.de

TABLE OF CONTENT

1 Software Development Project Risk Management –
Enhancement of Existing Theories
Chul-Young Byun 1

2 The Role of the Compliance Officer - a Comparison
of U.S., U.K. and German Law and Practice
Katrin Kanzenbach 33

3 Critical analysis of the precision of valuations
in financial experts' fairness opinions
Tobias Lippe 71

4 Social comparison as a mediator variable
between communication design and purchase intention
Agnieszka Michniuk 91

5 Digitalization and Motion Pictures:
A Theatrical Market Analysis
Florian Wrobel 117

The Authors 141
The Supervisors 145

1
SOFTWARE DEVELOPMENT PROJECT RISK MANAGEMENT – ENHANCEMENT OF EXISTING THEORIES

Chul-Young Byun

TABLE OF CONTENT

1.1 Introduction 3
1.2 Risks in non-agile and agile projects 5
    1.2.1 Sensitization of the thematic context 5
    1.2.2 Basic definitions 6
1.3 Research areas 12
    1.3.1 Risk factors for non-agile and agile projects 12
    1.3.2 Risk management for non-agile and agile projects 13
1.4 Project risk factor related theories 14
    1.4.1 Project risk management theory 14
    1.4.2 Information economics theory 15
    1.4.3 Principal agent theory 16
    1.4.4 Bounded rationality theory 17
    1.4.5 Heuristics theory 18
1.5 Identification of a theory gap 20
1.6 Theory suggestion to reduce the theory gap 22
    1.6.1 Focusing on the present 22
    1.6.2 Present indicators of future risk factors 24
    1.6.3 Risk factor indicators based framework 25
1.7 Conclusion 27
References 28

1.1 INTRODUCTION

It is not a successful strategy to run away from risks. Software development projects – especially where the project deliverables are huge and complex software systems – are exposed to high risks. (Barki, Rivard and Talbot, 2001; Schmidt et al., 2001; Takagi, Mizuno and Kikuno, 2005; Tharwon, 2011; Wallace, Keil and Rai, 2004) In Table 1 some huger failures of software development and rollout projects are shown, which underlines how challenging such projects could be. (Wallmüller, 2004)

Project	Delay	Loss
German „Toll collect"	2 years	€ 2200 mio
„YOU" Project by Bank Vontobel	Abortion after 2 years	€ 210 mio
California Car Registration	3 years	€ 41 mio
American Airlines Car Rental	7 years	€ 126 mio
Denver Airport Luggage Distribution	2 years	€ 573 mio
US Federal Tax Office	8 years	€ 1223 mio
London, Electronic Stock Market	12 years	€ 937 mio
London, Ambulance Guidance System	5 years	€ 14 mio and loss of 46 human lives

Table 1: Project Disasters (adapted from Wallmüller (2004)).

In order to have higher chances to complete a project successfully in terms of time and cost it is required to recognize risks or potential problems early and to address them. (Wallmüller, 2004) However, Kutsch and Hall (2009) found out that due to cost justification for around every third project out of around 100 examined IT projects there was basically no formal project risk management applied. (Kutsch and Hall, 2009) Another negative factor is that in many cases where project risk management is applied it is less effective because it is mostly done without committed senior management, which is crucial for effective project risk management. (Kaliprasad, 2006; Schmidt et al., 2001; Shan Liu et al., 2010) One arising question is how to handle a situation facing such negative factors.

One aspect of the answer is agile project management. Not necessarily due to the challenges to apply project risk management appropriately but due to the common goal of completing projects successfully at least with the Agile Manifesto in 2001 (Beck et al., 2001) agile project management started to become a trend in the project management area. The agile project management methodology emphasizes an iterative approach with high focus on short iteration cycles and team commitment, team accountability and team self-organization. (Sutherland and Schwaber, 2007) It could be deduced that due to that high focus on short iteration cycles and full team enablement many project risks are implicitly addressed and that therefore it could make sense not to apply traditional project risk management practices within an iteration or an agile project. In other words, there could be an understanding that agile project management does not need traditional project risk management. However, also agile projects are exposed to risks as non-agile projects are. Therefore, it would make sense to have a project risk management methodology for agile projects as well, especially if a project is not fully applying the agile project management methodology. The question is whether it would be necessary to have two different kind project risk management just due to the fact whether a project is following an agile or a non-agile approach or whether it would be possible to formulate one common framework for project risk management regardless which of both project methodologies is used.

This article provides an overview of project risk management related theories, describes an identified theory gap around project risk management for agile as well as non-agile projects, suggest a new theory how to bridge the identified theory gap and provides a suggestion of a framework for risk management for software development projects ranging from agile to non-agile methodologies.

1.2 RISKS IN NON-AGILE AND AGILE PROJECTS

This chapter provides a sensitization on relationships between the areas of risks, uncertainties, projects, non-agile (plan-driven) project management methodologies, agile (change-driven) project management methods as well as project risk management.

1.2.1 SENSITIZATION OF THE THEMATIC CONTEXT

It can be stated that projects are exposed to uncertainties including risks. Assumptions are made before or during a project and actions are taken under different degrees of uncertainty. Risks, which are a subset of uncertainties, can endanger the success of a project if such risks have negative impacts on a project. Project risk management techniques aim to mitigate risks in order to increase the chances of a successful project completion. (Wallmüller, 2004) Figure 1 provides a graphical presentation of the relationships between projects, uncertainties and risks.

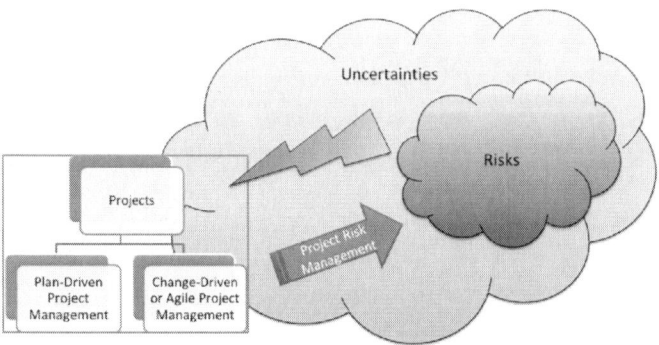

Figure 1: Projects and Risks

It should be noted that a project could be managed more plan-driven (basically first fully plan and then fully execute) or more change-driven (basically do not plan too much but at least good enough, execute and embrace changes). (Highsmith, 2010) Such distinction is necessary to mention because the plan-driven methodology and the change-driven methodology have different approaches to risk handling. Therefore they have different project risk management profiles, which are described in the next section along with the definitions of further necessary terms.

1.2.2 BASIS DEFINITIONS

1.2.2.1 PROJECT

The term project is a crucial term for this article and therefore it is important to have a clear definition about what a project is. There exist several definitions of the term project. The definition per PMI (2008) is that a project is "a temporary endeavor undertaken to create a unique product, service or result". (Project Management Institute, 2008) Per the APICS dictionary (2010) project is "an endeavor with a specific objective to be met within predetermined time and dollar limitations and that has been assigned for definition or execution". (Blackstone, 2010) Both definitions are similar but one difference is that the APICS dictionary also reflects aspects around cost in its definition. However, in course of this article it is sufficient to use the more generic definition of PMI.

1.2.2.2 PLAN-DRIVEN PROJECT MANAGEMENT

The methodologies of managing projects have evolved over time. Today, the "traditional" project management could be considered as "plan-driven" project management. The description "plan-driven" is used in order to distinguish from the recent trend in project management, which is the "change-driven" or "agile" project management, which will be defined later.

Per PMI (2008) project management is "the application of knowledge, skills, tools, and techniques to project activities to meet the project requirements". (Project Management Institute, 2008)

Per Wallmüller (2004) a project controls risks and problems via project management where risk management is a discipline of project management. Project management can be then assumed as planning, operating, controlling and organizing of a project. Project goals, timelines, resources, organization and culture are some project management areas. Furthermore, a project follows project management processes like for example project start, project controlling, project crisis management, project phase transition and project closure. (Wallmüller, 2004)

Per Highsmith (2010) plan-driven project management could be defined as "project management processes and practice" emphasizing "complete early planning and requirements specification with minimal ongoing change". (Highsmith, 2010)

Among these three definitions the one of PMI is too generic for the purpose of this article as it could be applied to plan-driven as well as agile projects. The remaining two definitions i.e. Wallmüller's and Highsmith's definitions offer more aspects of a plan-driven project management approach as they include project phases. However, in contrast to Wallmüller's definition Highsmith's definition includes beside project phase aspects the assumption that ongoing change is expected to be minimal. Therefore, Highsmith's definition, which states "plan-driven" project management as processes and practices, which emphasize completion of early planning and requirements specification with "minimal ongoing change", is used in course of this article.

1.2.2.3 CHANGE-DRIVEN (OR AGILE) PROJECT MANAGEMENT

Planning is a crucial aspect for "change-driven" project management, but the emphasis is higher on being flexible regarding ongoing changes. (Highsmith, 2010; Hoda, Noble and Marshall, 2011; Sutherland and Schwaber, 2007) Highsmith (2010), Hoda (2011) and Sutherland (2007) are providing definitions on "change-driven" project management. However, in course of this article Highsmith's (2010) definition is selected as it also covers the other definitions. Highsmith (2010) defines "change-driven" project management as processes and practices emphasizing "nominal early planning, good enough requirements, and experimental and evolutionary design with significant ongoing learning and change". (Highsmith, 2010)

1.2.2.4 RISK AND UNCERTAINTY

Because of the longer tradition of the term risk a broad spectrum of different understandings have been evolved. Many of these understandings are rooted in different continuously changed beliefs and convictions of the past hundreds of years of human culture. It has been about 350 years where the old belief that the future is defined by divine rule has been started to be switched to the today's widespread probability theoretical thoughts. Therefore, there are many definitions of the term risk. However, none of them are generally accepted. (Wallmüller, 2004; Wencke Schröder, 2005) For this article the definitions of Galbraith (1977), Kaliprasad's (2006), Kerzner (2006), Krane et al. (2010) and PMI (2008) have been analyzed. For the term risk the definition of Krane et al. (2010) has been selected, and for the term uncertainty a combination of Krane et al.'s (2010) and Kaliprasad's (2006) definition has been taken. Krane et al. (2010) defines risk as an uncertain event that, if it occurs, has an effect on an area of interest and the combined definition of Krane et al.'s (2010) and Kaliprasad's (2006) on uncertainty can be described as a future event with impact on an area of interest, where the occurrence probability of the impact of the future event on the area of interest and/or occurrence probability of the future event are not known.

1.2.2.5 STANDARD PROJECT RISK MANAGEMENT PROCESS

There exist several approaches with different focuses on how to do project risk management. An overview of standards and processes around risk management distinguishing between project risk management and organization risk management is provided by Raz and Hillson (2005). Besides Raz and Hillson's (2005) overview it is worth to add a process description presented by Carbone and Tippett (2004), which is an extension of the Failure Mode and Effects Analysis (FMEA) format. These descriptions span a range of project risk management processes concepts. For this article the definition of PMI (2008) in the PMBOK has been selected. Per that definition of PMI (2008) the project risk management process consists of 6 steps (see Figure 2).

Figure 2: PMBOK Project Risk Management Processes.

1.2.2.6 RISK FACTOR

The last important term for the new project risk management concept is the term risk factor. Sometimes the terms risk and risk factor are referred as the same, but for this article it is crucial to distinguish both terms. Schmidt et al. (2001) define a risk factor as "a condition that can present a serious threat to the successful completion of a software development project". (Schmidt et al., 2001) This definition provided by Schmidt et al. (2001) is addressing all necessary aspects. Based on that definition certain conclusions can be made regarding risk factors. As risk factors are influencing risks in the sense of increasing the risk occurrence probability and/or the negative impact of the risk it could be stated that a risk factor is timeline wise occurring earlier than the risk influenced by that risk factor. Therefore, such a risk factor can occur in the future but there is no limitation on that such a risk factor can also occur in the present or in the past. However, if a risk factor occurred in the past or occurs in the present that risk factor must not be necessarily considered as a problem if it does not endanger the present. Therefore, past and present risk factors, which are also perceived as problems, can be treated by problem management, and past and present risk factors, which are not perceived as problems, can be treated by risk management. The latter case underlines that managing risk factors means indirectly managing risks because of the interrelationship between risk factors and risks. Such a focus to present risk factors and in general to the present is one crucial new aspect in regards to project risk management. This is further described in the following sections.

1.3 RESEARCH AREAS

One problem is that software development projects are struggling with the fact that software development projects are complex and hard to predict. (Schwaber, 2010) One arising question could be how a project risk management framework could look like regardless of the applied project management methodology, be it non-agile or agile. One possibility could be to extend the current project risk management theory with a higher focus on risk factors rather than on risks. This leads to two research areas as described below.

1.3.1 RISK FACTORS FOR NON-AGILE AND AGILE PROJECTS

Project risk factors contribute to project risks. In the literature there exist several studies regarding top risks and top risk factors of software development projects. (Barki, Rivard and Talbot, 2001; Krane, Rolstadås and Olsson, 2010; Schmidt et al., 2001; Shan Liu et al., 2010; Tesch, Kloppenborg and Frolick, 2007; Tharwon, 2011; Tiwana and Keil, 2004) However, it should be noticed that these studies of Barki, Rivard and Talbot (2001), Krane, Rolstadås and Olsson (2010), Schmidt et al. (2001), Shan Liu et al. (2010), Tesch, Kloppenborg and Frolick (2007), Tharwon (2011) and Tiwana and Keil (2004) were made in parallel of the agile project management trend and it is not clear whether these studies have distinguished between non-agile and agile projects. Therefore, one research area is the determination of the current top risk factors for non-agile (plan-driven) and agile (change-driven) projects. Such a list of risk factors forms a critical input for a risk factor indicators based software development project risk management framework.

1.3.2 RISK MANAGEMENT FOR NON-AGILE AND AGILE PROJECTS

One major intention of agile projects is to provide the project deliverables iteratively, where an iteration last in general one to four weeks. (Sutherland and Schwaber, 2007) Due to such short iteration cycles it does not seem to be efficient to apply formal project risk management practices within such iteration. In addition, as the agile approach fosters a strong attitude of each team member to be focused only on the current iteration work and deliverables and to proactively help out other team members as much as possible it is assumed that any issues as well as any risks endangering the deliverables of the agile project are intrinsically addressed. In other words, risk management is an intrinsic part of each team member's daily project iteration work. Therefore, traditional project risk management could be less considered to be applied in agile projects rather than in non-agile projects. A research question would be then how a risk factor indicators based project risk management framework can serve as a common risk management framework for non-agile projects as well as agile projects.

1.4 Project Risk Factor Related Theories

In this chapter it is presented how various theories are related to the already existing risk factor checklist concept for projects, and it is described which theories supports the theory around a project risk management framework for software development projects ranging from non-agile to agile methodologies based on utilizing the strengths of the risk factor checklist concept.

1.4.1 Project Risk Management Theory

To state the obvious, the project manager is involved on the project level in regards to project risk management. The project portfolio management (PPM) is involved on the project portfolio level, and the project management office (PMO) is involved from a project process and quality perspective.

The risk register is used by the project manager to track the risks. The risk register can be used as risk communication tool between the project manager and PPM. In more mature organizations the PMO would be responsible for standardization around project risk management processes and tools.

As project risk factors are contributing to project risks there is a clear relationship between risk factors and a risk register.

Like for risk registers a template could be formulated also for risk factor checklists. Such a template would be maintained by the PMO whereas the risk factor checklist itself would be managed project specifically by the project manager. PPM would be similarly involved with risk factor checklists as with risk registers.

In summary, it can be stated that there is a relationship between risk factors and risks listed in a risk register, and that there is interaction regarding the risk factor checklist between the project manager, PPM and the PMO. By this the risk factor checklist concept is part of the project risk management theory. All relationships are pictured in Figure 3.

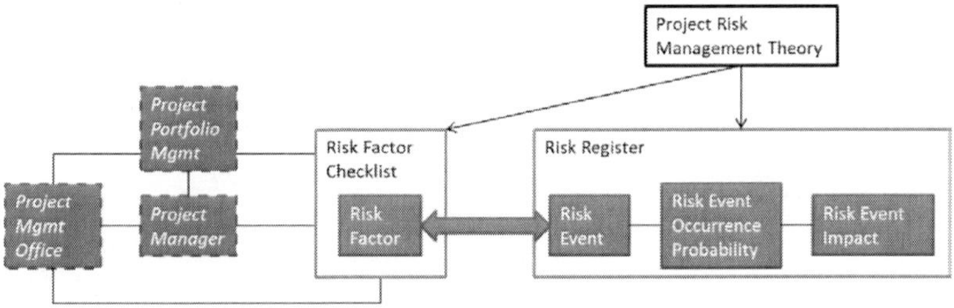

Figure 3: Relationship with Project Risk Management Theory.

1.4.2 INFORMATION ECONOMICS THEORY

The information economics theory extends the theory of the uncertainty economics theory mostly around information and knowledge. One different assumption of the information economics theory in contrast to the uncertainty economics theory is that in the information economics theory knowledge is determined by activities of the individual at the market and is not simply a given. (Arrow, 1984) Thus, the knowledge of an individual is influenced by the individual's activities within the model and is not influenced anymore by "external" model inputs. This has led to extensive explanations around the economical optimum and the arrangement of obtaining and transferring information. (Arrow, 1984) Typical related theoretical areas are search cost, information values, screening, signaling, self-selection, etc. (Arrow, 1984; Hirshleifer, 1973; Marschak, 1974; Spence, 1974; Stigler, 1961; Stiglitz, 1974).

In the area of project risk management the relationship between the PMO and a project manager could be described via the information economics theory. The maintenance of the risk factor checklist is under the responsibility of the project manager. Via the risk factor checklist the project manager is providing information ("signaling"), which is evaluated by the PMO ("screening") in order to reduce the "information asymmetry". Hence, it could be stated that there is a relationship between the information economics theory and the risk factor checklist concept (see Figure 4).

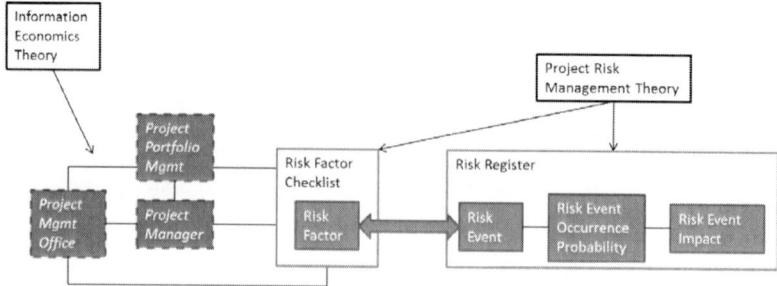

Figure 4: Relationship with Information Economics Theory.

1.4.3 PRINCIPAL AGENT THEORY

The problem and the handling of such in regards to the contractual relationship between two parties are addressed by the principal agent theory. In that theory one party ("agent") acts on behalf of the other ("principal"). Both parties have different interest and different level of information ("asymmetric information"). Usually, the principal has less information than the agent. The theory states that the agent could utilize such an advantage of asymmetric information to deviate from the principal best interest in order to satisfy the agent's self-interest. Such deviation is called agency cost. (Eisenhardt, 1989; Fama and Jensen, 1983a, 1983b; Laux, 1990)

In the area of project risk management the relationship between the PMO and a project manager could be described by the principal agency theory as the PMO and the project manager have directly or indirectly a contractual relationship. The project manager, who would be the agent, is asked by the PMO, which would be the principal, to provide information about project risk factors. It could be that the project manager's perception of project risk factors differs from the perception of the PMO. For example the project manager evaluates a risk factor less critical than the PMO would have evaluated it, but this fact could be one, which is recognized by the project manager but not by the PMO. This could lead to a deviation of the PMO's best interest as the PMO would not be able to intervene per the PMO's self-interest. Based on the principal agent theory such deviation would form the agency cost as described by Eisenhardt (1989), Fama and Jensen (1983a, 1983b) or Laux (1990). In summary, it could be stated that the principal agent theory has a relationship with the risk factor checklist concept (see Figure 5).

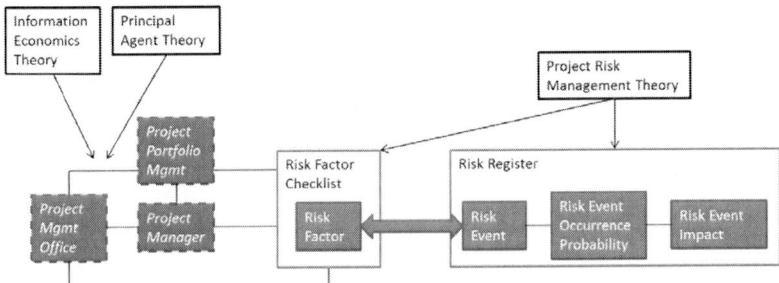

Figure 5: Relationship with Principal Agent Theory.

1.4.4 BOUNDED RATIONALITY THEORY

The behavior in the decision making process, where neither full rationality nor full irrationality is assumed, is explained by the bounded rationality theory. This theory considers that (1) an individual is limitedly rational, that (2) an individual is satisfied with what suffice ("satisfice") meaning an individual is aiming to satisfice rather than to maximize, that (3) an individual can change aspiration levels through learning and own actions, and that (4) an individual takes a decision based on the individual's aspiration level. (Simon, 1955, 1956, 1993).

The traditional project risk management theory assumes human rationality or the "homo oeconomicus", and therefore, it is also exposed to the criticism by the bounded rationality theory. This actually links project risk management theory aspects with the bounded rationality theory (see Figure 6).

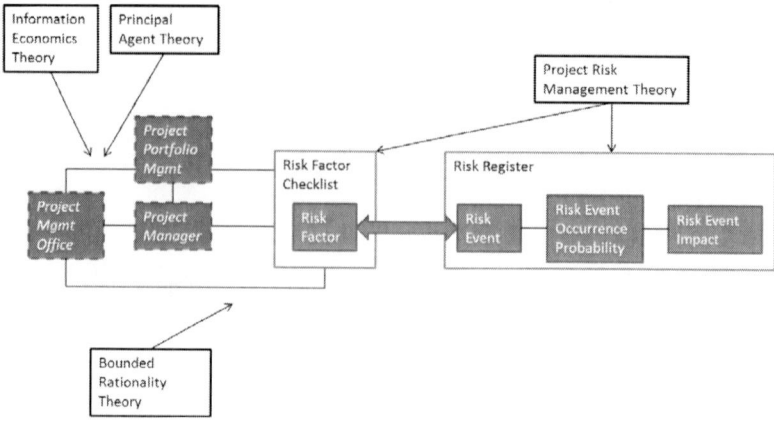

Figure 6: Relationship with Bounded Rationality Theory.

It should be noted that decisions under bounded rationality are not necessarily bad decisions. The theory of bounded rationality has opened several research paths around how to obtain faster good or good enough results in a less ideal environment. In such a less ideal environment for example not all information is available, or there are boundaries on time and resources to determine an optimal solution or human beings cannot or are not able to make full rational decisions. One of these research paths opened by the bounded rationality theory is the theory around heuristics, which is described in the next section.

1.4.5 HEURISTICS THEORY

The word heuristic stems from the Greek verb "to find" or "to discover". (Gigerenzer and Gaissmaier, 2006) The target of a heuristic is to find or to discover a solution to a given problem. Streim (1975) provides three general characteristics of heuristics so that heuristics can be better distinguish from other kinds of problem solution finding methods. (Streim, 1975) The first characteristic is that it follows a non-discretionary solution finding approach. The second characteristic is that due to the first characteristic heuristics are overlooking potential solutions. The third characteristic is that heuristics do not have an optimal solution convergence proof. These three characteristics are driven by the need to find good enough solutions while respecting time and resource constraints on the solution finding process. Due to this capability of finding good enough solutions efficiently heuristics can be identified in many scientific disciplines like for example in economics, in psychology, in computer sciences, in natural sciences or in mathematics. (Colman, 2006; Gall, 1996; Hertwig, 2006; Sutherland, 1989)

In the area of project risk management a systematic approach would mean to consider every possible risk. However, the management of every possible risk can easily lead to be a costly activity. In the project risk management area a heuristics based approach could be considered to be used as the heuristic theory supports a less systematic approach, which is perhaps less effective but effective enough, and which due to the strong focus on efficiency respects the limitation on time and cost. So, for example, the usage of a pre-defined risk or risk factor checklist is a less effective but a more efficient method. This is backed up by the general heuristic theory. Therefore, there is a relationship of the general heuristics theory with the risk factor checklist concept (see Figure 7).

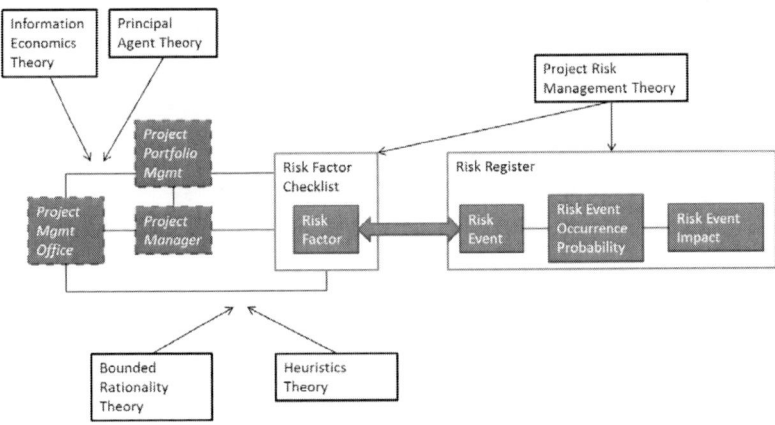

Figure 7: Relationship with Heuristics Theory.

1.5 Identification Of A Theory Gap

Even though it is recommended to apply project risk management a survey in 2009 revealed that in over one third of examined projects no formal project risk was applied due to cost justification. (Kutsch and Hall, 2009; Wallmüller, 2004) A possible other reason not to apply risk management in for example agile projects is that agile methodologies do not seem to foster formal project risk management due to the high focus on the current iteration, which is usually one to four weeks long, assuming that such focus on the present and near future addresses risks implicitly. Having the trend of agile methodologies in mind the (1) application of agile methodologies and (2) project cost justification are forming the basis and motivation for further research in the area of an efficient project risk management framework, which could be applied to projects ranging from agile to non-agile methodologies.

One possibility to address the cost justification factor is the utilization of risk checklists. Checklists have the benefit that their usage is more time and cost efficient due to the higher utilization of past experiences and knowledge. The disadvantage is that new or certain project specific risks are not covered through risk checklists. However, that disadvantage seems to be justified by the time and cost savings through the utilization of risk checklists rather than the utilization of time and cost consuming risk registers. A further time and cost saving leverage would be to focus the content of the checklist only to risk factors rather than on risks. The time and cost saving leverage would stem from the fact of focusing on risk factors and with this on the nearer future rather than on risks, which are usually in the farer future as they are per definition driven by risk factors. However, the focus on risk factors would be still a focus on the future. Therefore, a more present time centric view is missing or forming a gap in the state-of-the-art theory on project risk management (see Figure 8).

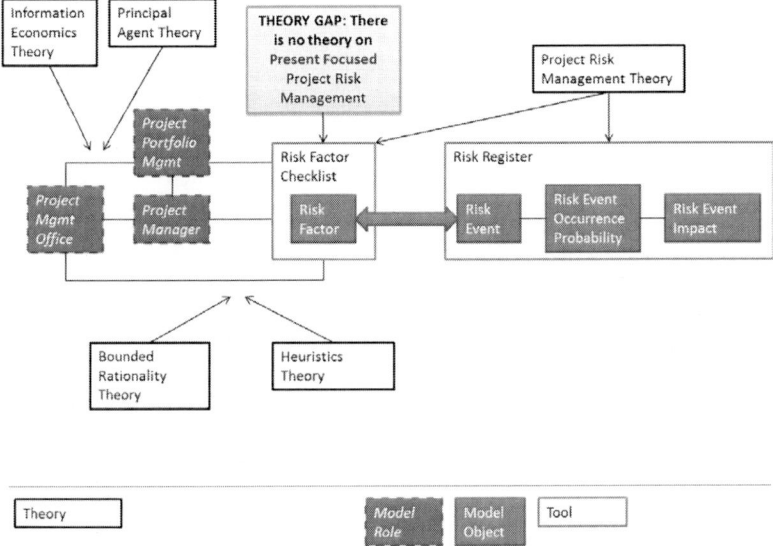

Figure 8: Identified Theory Gap in the Area of Risk Factor Based Risk Management.

This article aims to further close this theoretical gap as this would not only address the cost justification factor of not applying project risk management but would also address the application of agile methodologies factor of not applying project risk management.

1.6 THEORY SUGGESTION TO REDUCE THE THEORY GAP

There are several existing theories, which have a relationship with the risk factor concept. Two of those theories presented earlier in this article, namely the bounded rationality theory and the general heuristics theory, in combination with the weak signals theory by Ansoff are used to establish the theory of the risk factor indicator based project risk management (see Figure 9).

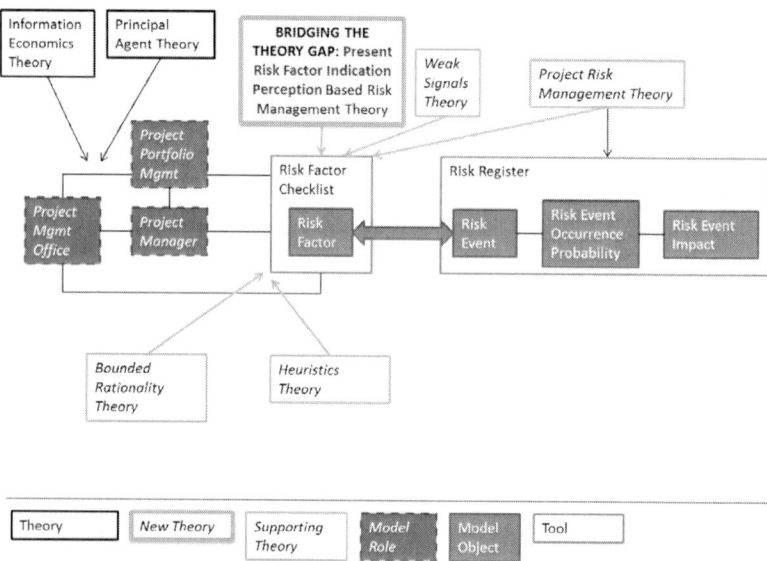

Figure 9: New Theory with Supporting Theories.

1.6.1 FOCUSING ON THE PRESENT

Today, the existing project risk management theory is concentrated on events, which could occur in the future. One new theoretical aspect is to expand the view of project risk management to the present time. It is actually about shifting the focus to the present or to present events. Present events can be in fact represented by two project risk management theory model objects. One of them is the present risk factor and the other one is the indicator of a future risk factor or a risk. If a present event is perceived as a risk factor or as a risk then actions can be engaged in order to address that present event and by this to indirectly address risks. It might be argued that present events are addressed by problem management. However, present events, which are present risk factors or which are present indicators of future risk factors or of future risks, are not necessarily problems. Therefore, dragging the focus to such present events, which are not problems and which are indicators of future risk factors or risks (see Figure 10), is a new theoretical aspect in the area of the project risk management theory.

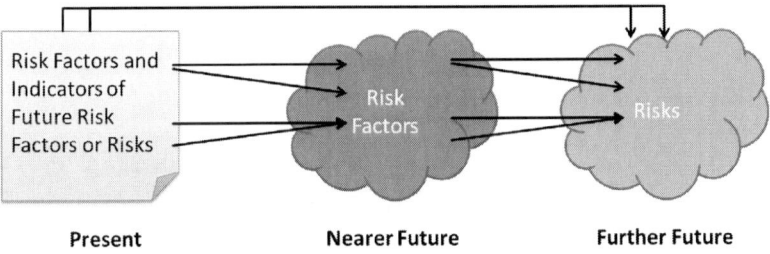

Present   **Nearer Future**   **Further Future**

Figure 10: Present Events Driving Risk Factors and/or Risks.

The sole focus on present events is backed up by the bounded rationality theory and the general heuristics theory. It has been earlier described that the bounded rationality theory is criticizing the assumption of the "homo oeconomicus" or in other words is criticizing the assumption of full human rationality. As the project risk management theory is assuming full human rationality the criticism of the bounded rationality theory can be also applied on the project risk management theory. It has been earlier described that the bounded rationality theory has led to several theories and research programs stating that decisions based on bounded rational judgment are not necessarily bad. Such theories and research programs are describing how good results can be quicker obtained even or especially in a less ideal or strict environment, where not all information is available, where time and resources to find an optimal solution are limited and where it is not possible for individuals to make ideal or optimal decisions. One of those theories is the heuristic theory. The heuristic theory can point to good enough alternative means to achieve results in such challenging environments. Therefore, it could be stated that the bounded rationality theory and the heuristics theory support the focus on present events in the area of project risk management.

1.6.2 PRESENT INDICATORS OF FUTURE RISK FACTORS

Earlier it is described that a present event can represent a present risk factor or a present indicator of one or more future risk factors. It should be noted that the distinction between a present risk factor and a present indicator of future risk factors can be sometimes challenging if for example a present risk factor drives a future risk factor. In such a case the present risk factor could be also considered as a present indicator of that future risk factor at the same time. Hence there exist a joint set of present risk factors and present risk factor indicators (see Figure 11).

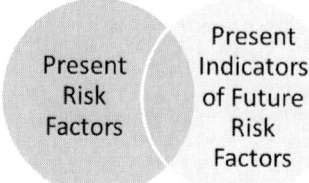

Figure 11: Present Risk Factors vs. Present Indicators of Future Risk Factors.

It is worth to make such distinction to better understand the composition of present events in the sense of project risk management and to be able to explain why it would be worth to exclude present risk factors moving forward. A present risk factor must have been actually a future risk factor before becoming a present risk factor. Therefore, such present risk factor must have been addressed by the already existing project risk management theory, where future risk factors are identified and appropriately mitigated. By this only present indicators of future risk factors remain, which are not covered by the project risk management theory.

One possible way of managing present indicators of future risk factors could be to identify and to manage them. However, it might well be that there are several indicators per risk factor. Hence, identifying and managing such indicators could mean a larger cost and time investment, which would ignore the findings in 2009 that in more than one third of projects no formal project risk was done due to cost justification. (Kutsch and Hall, 2009) Therefore, in order to actually address that finding a second new theoretical aspect comes into consideration. Instead of formally identifying and managing present indicators of future risk factors alternatively the perception of the project manager on the existence of such indicators would be used. Such an approach would be less time and cost consuming, which would address the findings mentioned earlier. Such an approach is backed up by Ansoff's weak signals theory, where the project manager's perception would correspond to Ansoff's weak signals, which are forming the integral part of Ansoff's strategic early warning system. (Ansoff, 1981) As there is a universe of future risk factors it is essential of having a list of the most relevant future risk factors in order to keep the investment in project risk management to an appropriate minimum.

1.6.3 RISK FACTOR INDICATORS BASED FRAMEWORK

Based on the two new theoretical aspects, namely (1) the focus on the risk factor indicators and (2) managing them only via the project manager's perception on the existence of such risk factor indicators, the high level process for the risk factor indicator based project risk management framework would be as follows. (1) List suspected risk factor indicators and (2) intervene based on the suspected risk factor indicators (see Figure 12).

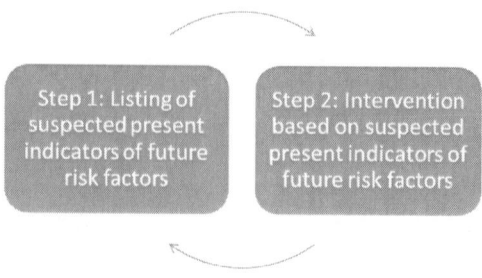

Figure 12: Framework Overview.

In order to make it more efficient a standard risk factor checklist concept should be used. That would extend the framework by a step 0, which is the establishment of a standard top risk factor checklist (see Figure 13).

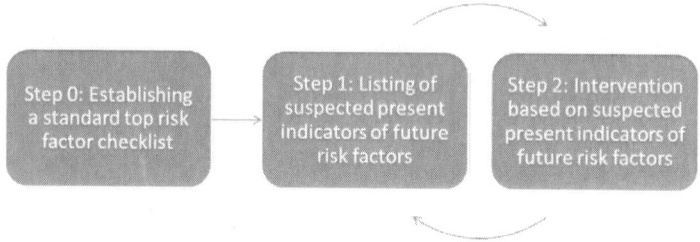

Figure 13: Extended Framework Overview.

Assuming that step 0 has been done or in other words assuming that a standard top risk factor checklist has been provided it would allow the project manager to start with step 1, where the project manager is providing feedback on each provided risk factor whether in the project manager's perception (a) there exist already present indicators, (b) whether there might be present indicators or (c) whether there do not exist any present indicators.

In step 2 the project manager is provided with a list of ranked risk factors based on the project manager's feedback on their suspected indications. This allows the project manager to intervene at the project manager's discretion depending on the specific project environment.

1.7 Conclusion

In this article it has been presented how project risk management theories are related to other theories. An analysis of these theories revealed a theory gap around project risk management for agile as well as non-agile projects. In order to bridge this identified theory gap a new theory has been formulated, which includes a basis for a risk management framework applicable to software development projects ranging from agile to non-agile methodologies.

One important critical input of such a framework is a standard risk factor list. Barki et al. (2001), Kaliprasad (2006) and Krane et al. (2010) have suggested what risks and risk factors should be considered for more effective project risk management, which is eventually suggesting on what kind of risks a project manager should pay higher attention. (Reed and Knight, 2010; Schmidt et al., 2001; Shan Liu et al., 2010; Tesch, Kloppenborg and Frolick, 2007; Tharwon, 2011; Tiwana and Keil, 2004)

However, these studies do not indicate whether a distinction was made between agile and non-agile projects. Therefore, one crucial activity is to obtain the view on standard risk factors from professional experts as well as academic experts via interviews in order to obtain an appropriate standard risk factor list. Once the framework has been established it is foreseen to validate the suggested framework via an experiment. The framework would be applied on experiment projects, which would be compared with control group projects. Such control group projects could be selected out of ongoing or completed projects, which are similar enough to the experiment projects. One possibility to compare the effect and efficiency of the suggested framework would be to survey the participating project managers how useful the suggested framework would have been for one or more of their completed projects.

Determining an appropriate standard risk factor list as well as the validation of the suggested framework via an experiment are the next steps in course of the doctoral research work.

REFERENCES

Ansoff, Harry I. (1981): "Die Bewältigung von Überraschungen und Diskontinuitäten: Strategische Reaktionen auf schwache Signale" In Planung und Kontrolle: Probleme der strategischen Untersuchungsführung, edited by Horst Steinmann. München: Vahlen, 1981.

Arrow, Kenneth J. (1984): The economics of information. Oxford: Blackwell, 1984.

Barki, Henri, Rivard, Suzanne, and Talbot, Jean (2001): "An Integrative Contingency Model of Software Project Risk Management" Journal of Management Information Systems 17, no. 4, 2001: p. 37–69. http://search.ebscohost.com/login.aspx?direct=true&db=buh&AN=4326034&lang=de&site=ehost-live.

Beck, Kent; Mike Beedle, Arie van Bennekum, Alistair Cockburn, Ward Cunningham, Martin Fowler, James Grenning, Jim Highsmith, Andrew Hunt, Ron Jeffries, Jon Kern, Brian Marick, Robert MartinC., Steve Mellor, Ken Schwaber, Jeff Sutherland, and Dave Thomas (2001): "Manifesto for Agile Software Development", 2001. http://agilemanifesto.org/, accessed 28-Sep-2011.

Blackstone, John H. (2010): APICS dictionary. 13th ed. Chicago, Ill: APICS, 2010.

Colman, Andrew M. (2006): A dictionary of psychology. Oxford [u.a.]: Oxford Univ. Press, 2006.

Eisenhardt, Kathleen M. (1989): "Agency Theory: An Assessment and Review" Academy of Management Review 14, no. 1, 1989: p. 57–74. http://search.ebscohost.com/login.aspx?direct=true&db=buh&AN=4279003&lang=de&site=ehost-live.

Fama, Eugene F., and Jensen, Michael C. (1983a): "Agency problems and residual claims" The Journal of Law & Economics 26, no. 2, 1983: p. 327–349.

Fama, Eugene F., and Jensen, Michael C. (1983b): "Separation of ownership and control" The Journal of Law & Economics 26, no. 2, 1983: p. 301–325.

Gall, Susan B. (1996): The Gale encyclopedia of psychology. Detroit: Gale, 1996.

Gigerenzer, Gerd, and Gaissmaier, Wolfgang (2006): "Denken und Urteilen unter Unsicherheit: Kognitive Heuristiken" In Enzyklopädie der Psychologie: C,II,8: Denken und Problemlösen, edited by J. Funke. Göttingen: Hogrefe, 2006.

Hertwig, Ralph (2006): "Strategien und Heuristiken" In Handbuch der Allgemeinen Psychologie - Kognition, edited by Joachim Funke. Göttingen [u.a.]: Hogrefe, 2006.

Highsmith, Jim (2010): Agile project management: Creating innovative products. 2nd ed. Upper Saddle River, NJ: Addison-Wesley, 2010.

Hirshleifer, Jack (1973): "Where are we in the theory of information" American Economic Review 63, no. 2, 1973: p. 31–39.

Hoda, Rashina, Noble, James, and Marshall, Stuart (2011): "Developing a grounded theory to explain the practices of self-organizing Agile teams" Empirical Software Engineering, 2011: p. 1–31.

Kaliprasad, Minnesh (2006): "Proactive Risk Management" Cost Engineering 48, no. 12, 2006: p. 26–36. http://search.ebscohost.com/login.aspx?direct=true&db=buh&AN=23594304&lang=de&site=ehost-live.

Krane, Hans P., Rolstadås, Asbjørn, and Olsson, Nils O. E. (2010): "Categorizing risks in seven large projects - Which risks do the projects focus on?" Project Management Journal 41, no. 1, 2010: p. 81–86.

Kutsch, Elmar, and Hall, Mark (2009): "The rational choice of not applying project risk management in information technology projects" Project Management Journal 40, no. 3, 2009: p. 72–81. 10.1002/pmj.20112.

Laux, Helmut (1990): Risiko, Anreiz und Kontrolle: Principal-Agent-Theorie; Einführung und Verbindung mit dem Delegationswert-Konzept. Berlin: Springer, 1990.

Marschak, Jacob (1974): "Ökonomische Probleme der Informationsgewinnung und- verwertung" In Mathematische Wirtschaftstheorie, edited by Martin J. Beckmann and Sato Ryuzo. Köln, 1974.

Projekt Management Institute (2008): A guide to the project management body of knowledge: PMBOK guide. Newtown Square, Pa: Project Management Inst, 2008.

Reed, April H., and Knight, Linda V. (2010): "PROJECT RISK DIFERENCES BETWEEN VIRTUAL AND CO-LOCATED TEAMS" Journal of Computer Information Systems 51, no. 1, 2010: p. 19–30. http://search.ebscohost.com/login.aspx?direct=true&db=buh&AN=54525525&lang=de&site=ehost-live.

Schmidt, Roy, Lyytinen, Kalle, Keil, Mark, and Cule, Paul (2001): "Identifying Software Project Risks: An International Delphi Study" Journal of Management Information Systems 17, no. 4, 2001: p. 5–36. http://search.ebscohost.com/login.aspx?direct=true&db=buh&AN=4326032&lang=de&site=ehost-live.

Schwaber, Ken (2010): Agiles Projektmanagement mit Scrum. 2nd ed. Unterschleißheim: Microsoft Press, 2010.

Shan Liu, Jinlong Zhang, Keil, Mark, and Tao Chen (2010): "Comparing senior executive and project manager perceptions of IT project risk: a Chinese Delphi study" Information Systems Journal 20, no. 4, 2010: p. 319–355. 10.1111/j.1365-2575.2009.00333.x.

Simon, Herbert A. (1955): "A BEHAVIORAL MODEL OF RATIONAL CHOICE" Quarterly Journal of Economics 69, no. 1, 1955: p. 99–118. http://search.ebscohost.com/login.aspx?direct=true&db=buh&AN=7704421&lang=de&site=ehost-live.

Simon, Herbert A. (1956): "Rational choice and the structure of the environment" Psychological Review 63, no. 2, 1956: p. 129–138.

Simon, Herbert A. (1993): Homo rationalis: Die Vernunft im menschlichen Leben. Frankfurt [u.a.]: Campus-Verl, 1993.

Spence, Michael (1974): "Competitive and optimal responses to signals: An analysis of efficiency and distribution" Journal of Economic Theory 7, no. 3, 1974: p. 296–332.

Stigler, G. J. (1961): "The economics of information" Journal of Political Economy 69, 1961: p. 213–225. http://search.ebscohost.com/login.aspx?direct=true&db=eoh&AN=1209161&lang=de&site=ehost-live.

Stiglitz, Joseph E. (1974): "Information and Economic Analysis" In Current Economic Problems, edited by Michael Parkin and A. R. Nobay. Manchester, 1974.

Streim, Hannes (1975): "Heuristische Lösungsverfahren Versuch einer Begriffsklärung" Zeitschrift für Operations Research 19, no. 5, 1975: p. 143–162.

Sutherland, Jeff, and Ken Schwaber (2007): "The Scrum Papers: Nuts, Bolts, and Origins of an Agile Process", Draft 10/14/2007, 2007. http://assets.scrumfoundation.com/downloads/2/scrumpapers.pdf?1285932052, accessed 13-Sep-2013.

Sutherland, Norman S. (1989): The International Dictionary of Psychology. New York: Continuum, 1989.

Takagi, Yasunari, Mizuno, Osamu, and Kikuno, Tohru (2005): "An Empirical Approach to Characterizing Risky Software Projects Based on Logistic Regression Analysis" Empirical Software Engineering 10, 2005: p. 495–515. http://dx.doi.org/10.1007/s10664-005-3864-z.

Tesch, Debbie, Kloppenborg, Timothy J., and Frolick, Mark N. (2007): "IT PROJECT RISK FACTORS: THE PROJECT MANAGEMENT PROFESSIONALS PERSPECTIVE" Journal of Computer Information Systems 47, no. 4, 2007: p. 61–69. http://search.ebscohost.com/login.aspx?direct=true&db=buh&AN=26000737&lang=de&site=ehost-live.

Tharwon, Arnuphaptrairong (2011): "Top Ten Lists of Software Project Risks : Evidence from the Literature Survey" Proceedings of the International MultiConference of Engineers and Computer Scientists 1, 2011: p. 732–737, accessed July 2012.

Tiwana, Amrit, and Keil, Mark (2004): "THE ONE-MINUTE RISK ASSESSMENT TOOL" Communications of the ACM 47, no. 11, 2004: p. 73–77. http://search.ebscohost.com/login.aspx?direct=true&db=buh&AN =14958359&lang=de&site=ehost-live.

Wallace, Linda, Keil, Mark, and Rai, Arun (2004): "How Software Project Risk Affects Project Performance: An Investigation of the Dimensions of Risk and an Exploratory Model" Decision Sciences 35, no. 2, 2004: p. 289–321. 10.1111/j.00117315.2004.02059.x.

Wallmüller, Ernest (2004): Risikomanagement für IT- und Software-Projekte: Ein Leitfaden für die Umsetzung in der Praxis. München: Hanser, 2004.

Wencke Schröder, Regina (2005): Risikoaggregation unter Beachtung der Abhängigkeiten zwischen Risiken. Zugl.: Witten, Herdecke, Univ., Diss., 2005. 1st ed. Baden-Baden: Nomos-Verl.-Ges, 2005.

2

THE ROLE OF THE COMPLIANCE OFFICER – A COMPARISON OF U.S., U.K. AND GERMAN LAW AND PRACTICE

Katrin Kanzenbach

TABLE OF CONTENT

2.1 Introduction 36
    2.1.1 Relevance of Problem Statement 37
    2.1.2 Objective and Research Questions 40
2.2 Methodology and Related Work 43
    2.2.1 Legal Comparison 43
    2.2.2 Interviews with Experts 44
    2.2.3 Literature Review 46
2.3 Analyses and Initial Results 50
    2.3.1 Roots and cultural background of Compliance in the US 50
    2.3.2 Roots and cultural background of Compliance in the UK 54
    2.3.3 Roots and cultural background of Compliance in Germany 58
2.4 Conclusion 63
References 65

ABSTRACT

This article responds to a problem outlined by many legal scholars and professionals concerning the establishment of a Compliance function within American, British, and German companies in the private sector. The assumption is that the role of Compliance must be clearly defined and organized. To date, however, the tasks and duties of the German Compliance Officer are unclear beyond the boundaries of the regulated financial sector and market. Thus, the main goal of my thesis is to establish a modern and standardized legal role and concept of the German Compliance Officer. The challenge is to ensure that the job description be tailored to a company's unique characteristics and providing the Compliance Officer with the requisite authority and tools. The present discussion focuses on how the role has evolved over the past 10 to 20 years. During this period in particular, the position of the Compliance Officer has changed dramatically. The legislation and statutory regulations put into place during this time have had a significant and far-reaching impact on companies today. As new requirements arise, so professional standards of the Compliance Officer will increase. A detailed analysis of the cultural background and legal roots of Compliance and Compliance Officers will be performed by reviewing the American, English, and German literature. The objective of the historical approach is to achieve a brief overview of where Compliance comes from in order to use this as the starting point for the development of a new modern role for this position. The historical understanding will lay the first milestone for the problem statement in my dissertation. In conclusion, the examination of the American, English, and German literature has revealed no cultural background and no legal definition of Compliance and Compliance Officers in the UK and Germany. Thus, it is no surprise that Compliance issues have been transferred from the US to the UK and Germany.

2.1 INTRODUCTION

In the course of the last century, companies across the globe have become involved with leading corporate efforts in Compliance.[1] With every new rule and the growing influence of government resolutions and agreements, the demands of Compliance are becoming more complex. In the US, for example, because of this specific development, organizations designate a "High-level position" or a "High-level personnel of the organization"[2] to oversee Compliance tasks and responsibilities. Increasingly often, this position is being referred to as "Chief Compliance Officer" or "Compliance Officer" (Ethics Resource Center, 2007, p. 6). Since 1990, the US has seen a significant increase in the attention afforded to this position (Weber & Fortun, 2005, p. 98). In comparison, the German academic discussion on Compliance and the Compliance function gained impetus in 2009 in the form of a decision of the Federal Supreme Court[3]. This case dealt with the Officer's responsibility within a company and integrated the still relatively novel company function "Compliance" into the German legal system.[4]

Over the past 20 years, the academic debate in the US has concentrated on future developments, on repositioning, on a structural reorganization of the Compliance function and the expertise of Compliance Officers (Greenberg, 2014; DeStefano, 2013; Taylor, 2006; Rosella & Pugliese, 2006). A second general theme arising from practice is the debate about the effectiveness of the Compliance Officer, the professional standards of this position, and its specific role (DeMott, 2013; Greenberg, 2009, Summary; Hoffman, et al., 2008b). Furthermore, there has been greater emphasis on the independence and impartiality of the Compliance Officer. It is proposed that reporting directly to the management

---

[1] The thesis will examine the function of the Compliance Officer in the private sector companies. The term private sector refers to the segment of the economy that is not controlled and not owned by the government. The private sector is run by individuals and companies. The entities that operate in the private sector are business enterprises, small and medium-size companies, and national, international, multinational corporations.
[2] US Sentencing Guidelines Manual, 2013, § 8A1.2., Commentary (2013) – *See*, available at: http://www.ussc.gov/training/organizational-guidelines/2013-ussc-guidelines-manual, (accessed: 28 March 2015).
[3] BGH, Urt. v. 17.7.2009 – 5 StR 394/08 - responsibility under criminal law on account of professional position.
[4] BGH, Urt. v. 17.7.2009 – 5 StR 394/08, at footnote 6, 19 ff.; BGH NJW 09, 3173.

would greatly enhance the Compliance Officer's independence, thereby reducing conflicts of interest (Gnazzo, 2011; Hoffman, et al., 2008b; Majewski, 2006).

However, the role of the Compliance Officer needs to be clearly defined and integrated within companies. The present article is structured as follows. Following a brief introduction, part two illustrates the relevance of the problem statement, its growth in importance over recent years and offers the research questions set out and raised in the present German discussion. Part three provides an overview of the literature relating to the American, British and German Compliance Officer and describes the methodical approach. The next part goes on to summarize the roots of American, British and German Compliance, the cultural background in each case, exploring the various specific descriptions of the term Compliance and presents initial results. The last part concludes with a summary of the similarities and differences between the American, British, and German legal roots of Compliance.

2.1.1 RELEVANCE OF PROBLEM STATEMENT

An examination of the German literature shows the following key topics concerning the Compliance function: What are the scope and the area of responsibility? Should the Compliance Officer be liable for any failure to detect misconduct by employees? Is the Compliance Officer able to limit his or her liability? Do Compliance Officers enjoy any protection against dismissal? How can the employment contract for a Compliance Officer best be designed (*See, e.g.* Schulz & Renz, 2012; Gößwein & Hohmann, 2011; Kirsch, 2011; Wolf, BB 2011; Nave, 2009; Wybitul, 2009)? The German legal environment that affects this function has been the subject of controversial debate. On the one hand, there is little uniformity and standardization of the Compliance function. A generally applicable definition of the Compliance function is still lacking (*See, e.g.* Wolf, 2011; Meier, 2011; Raus & Lützeler, 2012; Hauschka, 2014). These attitudes are inconsistent with the view taken by Groß, who counters that an entirely new and separate job description has developed in the meantime (Groß, 2012, p. 29). The actual practical debate within the German professional associations[5] represents the efforts

---

[5] *See, e.g.,* BCM Professional Association of Compliance Officers; BDCO German Federal Association of Compliance Officers.

to create a unique job description. In sum, it is acknowledged that there are many questions[6] concerning this position that have not yet been answered and there is a need for a generally applicable definition and a modern role concept for the German Compliance Officer.

Furthermore, Compliance Officers are often involved in administrative proceedings before the courts on account of their role in ensuring Compliance with the law and applicable rules within firms. On the one hand, the organizations are able to exercise the increased responsibility of the Compliance function, while on the other hand, a Compliance Officer needs a certain degree of political power, a legal framework within which to work, and standards to work to within the role (DeStefano, 2013, p. 82). Therefore, the main issues surrounding this function in terms of corporate law and labor law have demonstrated particularly unclear facts or uncertain legal situations.

There is a gap in knowledge between the far-reaching scope of the position and the limitation of the responsibilities of the Compliance function. According to Demott (2013, p. 56), the role and status of Compliance personnel have remained relatively unexamined by scholars, although there is a wide range of American[7] and German literature[8] and articles relating to the Compliance function. In Germany, the present situation of the Compliance Officer is characterized by a number of specific, unclear facts and an uncertain legal environment. As previously discussed, there has been a broad scientific discussion concerning the criminal duties and responsibilities of the post of Compliance Officer in the wake of the decision from the Federal Supreme Court.[9] It is precisely the legal position that is the most problematic aspect of the Compliance Officer's function. At present, the legal scope of action within which a German Compliance Officer works is widely undefined and the implementation thereof is not consistently standardized within the companies affected (Hauschka, 2014a, p. 243). Germany does not yet

---

[6] See supra p. 37.
[7] See, e.g., Gnazzo, Business and Society Review 2011; Greenberg, 2009; Pirraglia, Fordham Journal of Corp. & Fin. Law 2003; Freeman, Information Security Journal 2007, Fanto, Brooklyn Law Review 2013; De Stefano, Hastings Business L. J. 2013; Wolfe, Journ. of Fin. Regul. and Compliance 2004.
[8] See, e.g., Nave, BB 2009; Wybitul, BB 2009; Gößwein / Hohmann, BB 2011; Kirsch, BB 2011; Wolf, BB 2011; Schulz / Renz, BB 2012; Bürkle, Meier, NZA 2011, CCZ 2010; Lützeler, CCZ 2012; von Busekist, CCZ 2013; Hauschka, CCZ 2014; etc....
[9] BGH, Urt. v. 17.7.2009 – 5 StR 394/08 - responsibility under criminal law on account of professional position.

have a complete legal profile characterizing the work of a Compliance Officer. In summary, it is still lacking a *"standardized legal profile"* (Geiger, 2011, p. 170). Therefore, it could be useful to examine the legal environment for the Compliance function outside of Germany, as well as to explore their professional status within companies in other countries.

In the view of DeStefano (2013, p. 77), there has been little qualitative research[10] on Compliance Officers in the United States. In the German literature, such studies have not yet been published. Hence, my thesis will conduct interviews with Compliance Officers within companies. Such interviews could allow getting an insight into their day-to-day business. In addition, it will deliver a detailed legal comparison of the legal framework and the evolution of the Compliance function in the common law and civil law systems and will call for a shift in scholarly focus to look deeper within private-sector firms. More generally, the legal environment around the implementation of the formal function in the US, UK and Germany is the trigger behind the problem statement discussed in my thesis.

In conclusion, it can be stated that the discussion in the US focuses more on the recent and potential evolution of the role of Compliance Officer. The new role of the Compliance Officer has been redefined. In contrast, in Germany, the position gives more consideration to the structure and the legal status. Therefore, the purpose of my thesis is to combine these two different views and to establish the modern role of the Compliance Officer in Germany and their legal status. This goal could be achieved by analyzing the specialized nature of the Compliance Officers' in the common law and civil law systems. This objective will examine the following topics: the historical development of the Compliance function, the legal framework within which a Compliance Officer works, the contribution made by the Compliance function within private-sector firms, the conflicts in the role of Compliance Officers, the qualifications of Compliance Officers, the further evolution of this function and the implications thereof within companies in the common law and civil law systems. Lastly, professional standards, the modern role, and a concept of German Compliance Officers will be defined.

---

[10] *See, e.g.*, Hoffman, et al., 2008 – a sample of six interviewees of mutual fund Compliance Officers.

2.1.2 OBJECTIVES AND RESEARCH QUESTIONS

The primary goal of my doctoral thesis is to establish a modern and standardized profile of the German Compliance Officer with a concise description and definition of this function. This objective includes the description and evaluation of the responsibilities of the Compliance Officer, as well as an examination of their activities and the scope of the legal risks involved.

In addition, a large part of my dissertation will extensively research the range of duties and liabilities of Compliance Officers in private-sector companies. In America, the number of lawsuits against Officers is increasing year-on-year by between 15 and 20 percent (Chew, 1997, p. 2). Officers' liability includes the extension of liability, the risks of personal liability and many other potential kinds of liability. In the United States, the applicable Securities Laws legally define the individual liability of Compliance Officers. The Federal Securities Act of 1933 claims that *"every person who was a director of (or person performing similar functions)"* could be personally liable for certain activities.[11] One classification of personal liabilty was submitted by Traeger, et al (2014a). In fulfilling the Compliance Officers' function, Traeger, et al (2014a), identify three elements of individual liability: (1) a person violates the federal securities laws or rules, (2) this person is subject to the supervision of another individual, and (3) the supervising individual does not reasonably fulfill his or her supervisory responsibilities (p. 36).

The definition of which parties are to be classified as officers has not yet been satisfactorily settled. Notwithstanding numerous new provisions and defined legal terms, the law is not always clear. The risks and difficulties involved for the Officers, particularly for the Compliance Officer, determine their liability (Chew, 1997, p. 19).

Therefore, my research questions are framed as follows:

(1) How is the modern role and legal position of the Compliance Officer classified and defined in the common law and practice?

(2) Which aspects are transferable to the German Compliance Officer?

---

[11] Sec. 11 of the Securities Act 1933, Pub. L. 114-38, 15 U.S. Code § 77k (a) (2) - civil liability on account of false registration statement.

(3) How can the role of the German Compliance Officer be more effectively enhanced in practice?

The answers to these questions will be important for the German discussion[12] about this position relating to civil and criminal liability in the private-sector firms, both in theory and in practice. The results of this thesis could contribute to the evolution and change of the German Compliance function over the next few years. Furthermore, the findings of my thesis could be expanded upon to boost the understanding of the legal framework and environment of the Compliance function in the professional context.

In order to achieve the goals outlined above, I selected a comparison concerning the legal position and role of the Compliance Officer in the US, UK and Germany, based on academic debate in Germany. The investigation will focus on five aspects of the American, British and German Compliance Officer's role and legal position (1) the legal framework and contractual agreements in the respective jurisdiction pertaining to the function of Compliance Officers, (2) the Compliance Officer's wide range of purview, (3) the definition of the role of Compliance Officers, (4) a comparison of the corporate American, British and German Compliance role as a model for the Compliance professional, and (5) the aspects, which could be adopted for the German Compliance Officer. These considerations can be seen as the starting point for further research.

To achieve sustainable results, the methodological approach will conduct the following. At first, a legal comparison will perform and secondly a qualitative investigation will conduct. This investigation incorporates the goal of examining the legal framework of Compliance and of the Compliance function within companies in the common law and in the civil law systems. In addition, by analyzing and by evaluating the opinions in the literature, interviews will be carried out with American, British, and German Compliance Officers. The findings of these expert interviews could help to bring some much-needed clarity to the Compliance situation. Based on these findings, the study will then go on to describe and define the legal

---

[12] *See, e.g.,* Nave, BB 2009; Wybitul, BB 2009; Gößwein / Hohmann, BB 2011; Kirsch, BB 2011; Wolf, BB 2011; Schulz / Renz, BB 2012; Bürkle, Meier, NZA 2011, CCZ 2010; Lützeler, CCZ 2012; von Busekist, CCZ 2013; Hauschka, CCZ 2014; etc....

status and role of the Compliance Officer within German, British and US companies. An analysis of the data and the findings could serve to compile a modern role and model of legitimacy for the Compliance position.

In summary, that means it would be useful to perform an analysis of the differences and similarities in the legal framework and legal provisions of the two legal systems on the one hand, while on the other hand, the legal issues and case-law should be compared and the importance for legal developments identified.

2.2 METHODOLOGY AND RELATED WORK

2.2.1 LEGAL COMPARISON

This part determines the methods that constitute the basis of my thesis. Next, it leads to a review of related work concerning the Compliance function. Two different types of methods were used to examine the research questions. The first is a legal comparison and the second a qualitative method: the interviews with experts. Additionally, the historical legal background and social implications of the Compliance function will be presented.

The practice of comparing substantive laws and legal procedures is simultaneously *"very old"* and *"very modern"* (Hopt, 2006, p. 1162). The method of comparative law is *"old"* because trade has never stopped at the frontiers of countries and states. In this context, *"modern"* means comparative law has always been considered to be an enrichment of legal solutions (Hopt, 2006, pp. 1162-1167). Comparative law allows attorneys, legislators, and scholars to understand and learn from legal systems in foreign jurisdictions (Djilani, 2010, p. 303).

In the view of Zweigert and Kötz (1996), the origin of comparative law lies in the analysis of legal problems. The primary objective of comparative law is recognition (Zweigert & Kötz, 1996, p. 14). First, the essential elements of the foreign law should be outlined in national reports. Then, it follows a consideration of the legal comparison and a critical discussion. In conclusion, the findings facilitate and provide interpretations of the national law (Zweigert & Kötz, 1996, p. 6).

Other critical voices concluded that the functional method in comparative laws is an under theorized approach with an undefined disciplinary position (Michaels, 2005, p. 25). In Michaels' (2005) opinion, *"the functional method is strong as a tool for understanding, comparing, and critiquing different laws, but a weak tool for evaluating and unifying laws"* (p. 45). Thus, it appears that functionalist comparative law is not appropriate for unifying laws. However, it can be seen that this is not the aim of comparative law. We should look at an interpretive approach that integrates historical and cultural considerations. This would allow us to pick the best aspects from the common law system and could help to improve the legal framework in other legal jurisdictions. The difficult part is how to differentiate between "true" ("good") [...] and "false" ("bad"). The nature of the problem is that we cannot say that a foreign law is better than our own. Instead, we need to recognize different solutions in order to allow us to develop alternatives (Michaels, 2005, p. 43).

In brief, the research has to identify some common functions and characteristics of the American, British, and German Compliance Officers in order to establish a basis for a legal comparison. The comparison has to start with some definitions, to describe the regulatory framework in the US, UK and Germany, and to illustrate a few examples with a special focus on court decisions. Specifically, this means the scientific analysis and evaluation of the comparison of European corporate and labor law with the US law specifics and legal practice applicable to Compliance Officers will define the differences and similarities.

Based on this comparison of laws, tasks and powers for the Compliance Officers agreed upon in the employment agreements should be established. Understanding the respective roles and functions of American, British, and German Compliance Officers within companies will generally enable us to improve the recognition of this function and its position in private-sector companies. Finally, this comparative legal review will establish an organizational role for the German Compliance Officer.

2.2.2 Interviews with Experts

As explained previously, empirical knowledge about the role and legal position of Compliance Officer is limited.[13] Qualitative research has been underutilized for studying the legal status of this post. Qualitative methodology is appropriate for my thesis because empirical research in this area is at an early stage and the general research question is complicated and complex. According to Gläser & Laudel (2010), the qualitative researcher is interested in social perspectives or processes and perspectives (p. 13). Expert interviews could be a special method

---

[13] See supra p. 40.

of gaining specific knowledge about the Compliance Officers' area of business (Gläser & Laudel, 2010, p. 12).

Expert interviews are usually conducted in the form of semi-structured interviews, where the interviewer uses a prepared guideline (Gläser & Laudel, 2010, p. 111). The Compliance Officers could provide a perspective on their post and their experience from inside the companies. Stage one consists of 15 prepared semi-structured interviews, five with American corporate Compliance Officers, five with British corporate Compliance Officers, and five with German corporate Compliance Officers from large companies. The Compliance Officers represent private sector companies from various sectors. Hence, stage two will attempt to elicit relevant information about the working process, the working method, integration into the structure of the company, and future prospects by asking Compliance Officers directly.

Based on these interviews with present Compliance Officers, it can be expected to gain valuable information about the working environment, the structure, and implementation of employment contracts, the integration into the corporate structure, the internal reporting, and scope of responsibilities, authorities, and duties of Compliance Officers, etc.... The data gathered from these Compliance Officers can then be used as a complement to the legal comparison. Therefore, the hypotheses can be rejected or scientifically verified by a qualitative investigation of expert interviews with American, British, and German Compliance Officers within companies.

The first step of the legal comparison will reflect the American, British, and German legal framework pertaining to the position of Compliance Officer. In this context, the historical legal background and social developments will also be taken into consideration. The second step will explore the literature and articles relating to the key functions, *e.g.* the range of purview, liabilities, reporting, independence and special skills of the Compliance Officers. In addition, the interviews with the Compliance professionals will conduct for their insights in their day-to-day business. Hence, the answers will present a review of the variety of professional roles and skills. Beyond the review of the legal parameters and views of the post, the next step will be the research to establish the existing standards applicable to this profession. This approach can be helpful for defining in detail the position of Compliance in the fourth step. In conclusion, the previous investigation will prepare the basis for submitting a draft and guidelines for a new modern status of the German Compliance Officer. *Figure 1,* below, summarizes all of these points and facts:

```
                    Qualitative method:
                    Interviews with American, British
                    and German CO's for their insights

                              (5) A modern and efficient model of the German
                              Compliance Officer (Guidelines)

                              (4) A precise description and definition of the
                              German Compliance function

                              (3) Research for existing American, British and
                              German standards of this profession

                              (2) Investigation and review of the key role of
                              the American, British and German Compliance
                              Officer

                              (1) Legal Comparison of the legal framework,
                              judicial decisions and contractual agreements
                              in the respective jurisdiction

Special historical legal background        Relevant social relations and de-
in the US, UK and Germany                  velopments in the US, UK and Ger-
                                           many
```

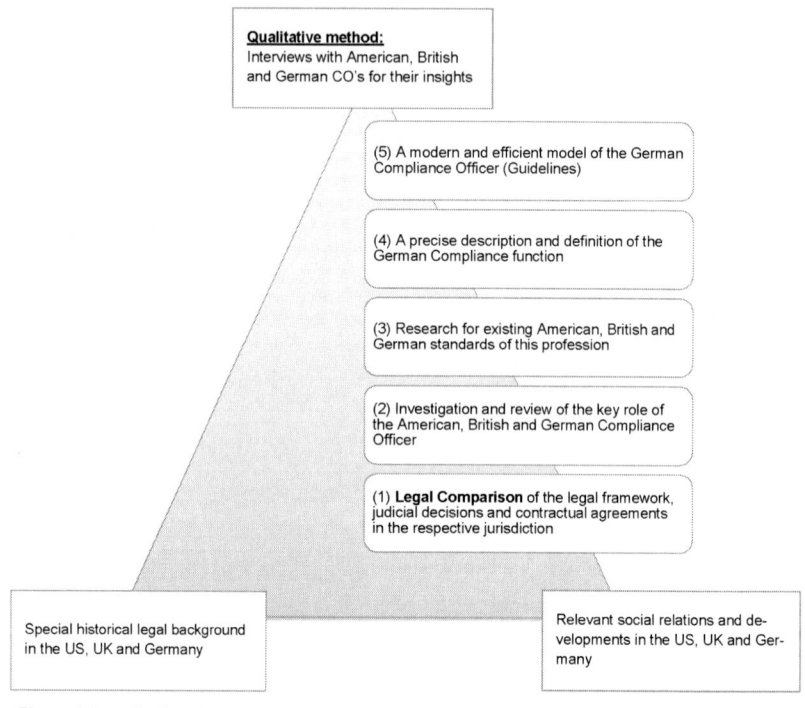

Figure 1: Investigation design of the thesis.

2.2.3 LITERATURE REVIEW

It has been recognized, that the academic discussion has become increasingly considered the organizational role of the Compliance function. The literature includes research related to the role and challenges of Compliance Officers (*See, e.g.,* Greenberg, 2010; Freeman, 2007; Taylor, 2006); Compliance Director liability (*e.g.,* Pirraglia, 2003); the evolving standard and professional development of Compliance personnel (*see, e.g.,* Greenberg, 2014; Fanto,

2013; Rosella & Pugliese, 2006; Meaney, 2001); and the effects of professionalism (*e.g.,* Rosen, et al., 2013).

By surveying the American, British and German literature, scholarly articles in journals, research papers, Compliance studies and Conference proceedings, the findings can be allocated to four categories: (1) the historical legal background, (2) the current statutory framework, (3) the critical analysis of the position of the Compliance Officer, and (4) the further evolution and standardization of this function. More generally, assessing the strengths and weaknesses of the Compliance function could help to define the Compliance position and to establish a modern and efficient model for the German Compliance Officer. Nevertheless, a legal comparison of the Compliance function is largely absent from the English and German literature. As a result, there is much that we still do not know about the new role and the potential liabilities of this function, about the standard for imposing liability, as well as the legal risks facing Compliance Officers.

There are some interviews, Compliance studies,[14] and surveys[15] with American leading Compliance professionals and Compliance practitioners that investigate issues similar to those set forth in my research questions (See, *e.g.,* PWC, 2014; Consero Group LLC., 2012; PWC, 2012; Weber & Fortun, 2005; Parker, 2000). Since 1922, the American non-profit organization Ethics Resource Center[16] has published many surveys and reports on current and emerging issues relating to Ethics and Compliance. The findings of these studies and interviews might help us to understand the specific role of the Compliance Officer within an organization.

In addition, the results of the American Compliance surveys and studies yield a classification of the Compliance professionals as *"dual-hatted"* individuals (Traeger, et al., 2014a) or even a *"dual role,"* because a Compliance Officer often holds multiple positions within a firm. According to a PWC study (2014),

---

[14] See, *e.g.,* available at http://www.pwc.com/us/stateofCompliance.
[15] See, *e.g.,* available at http://consero.com/2012-chief-Compliance-officer-data-survey/.
[16] The Ethics Resource Center (ERC) is America's oldest non-profit organization devoted to independent research and the advancement of high ethical standards and practices in public and private institutions. This organization provides recommendations to the Private Sector.

Compliance is an add-on responsibility for another function. 54 percent of respondents said that the Compliance function wears multiple hats. Often, this role is assumed by the General Counsel (PWC, 2014, p. 10). This development is viewed critically by DeStefano (2013). She claimed that the unofficial stance by the US Securities and Exchange Commission (SEC) and the Department of Health and Human Services (DHHS) is to separate the Compliance and Legal functions (DeStefano, 2013, p. 74). It seems as though the role of Compliance Officers should be clearly distinguished from other functions within companies. This could be another important starting point for defining and redefining this function.

The advantage arising from surveying the American literature is being able to trace the historical legal development of the Compliance function, to present a regulatory overview, to understand the organizational role, to define the Compliance Officer profile and a new standard, and its position for the future. It can be helpful to work out a precise description and definition and to design a modern role. In the US, the Federal Securities Law[17] requires a supervisory role of this function within the framework of the corporate structure.[18] A supervisory role means the duty to reasonably oversee subordinates and ensure subordinates' compliance with the Securities Laws.[19] One question that has been raised and discussed at length over the past few years is: When is a Compliance professional a "*supervisor*" under the Federal Securities Laws? (Traeger, et al., 2014a, p. 25). The Compliance personnel were viewed as the "*first line of defense*" or "*gatekeepers of Compliance*" (Traeger, et al., 2014a, p. 25; DeStefano, 2013, p. 75). In other words, a Compliance Officer needs, for example, to implement, monitor, audit and oversee an effective Compliance Program in companies as well as to conduct screenings to avoid hiring employees that have been sanctioned in the passed. On the other hand, the Officer should build alliances with the key stakeholders, such as Legal, Human Resources, Finance and Accounting, as well as business operations.

---

[17] In response to the financial crisis, the collapse of financial markets and the Depression of the 1930s, the US government enacted the Securities Acts of 1933 and 1934 and other regulatory enactments.
[18] 15 USC. § 78o (1990) - United States Code, 1990 Edition, Title 15 - COMMERCE AND TRADE *See*, available under: http://uscode.house.gov/, (accessed: 28 March 2015).
[19] *Ibid.*

In conclusion, the combined evaluation of the specific and complex nature of the Compliance function with the resulting supervisory duties and legal liabilities will be a topic for further research in the course of my dissertation. The detailed reflection of the literature and the findings from the interviews could help to contribute to a clear classification, a transparent job description, a standardized legal profile, and approach of the Compliance Officer.

2.3 ANALYSES AND INITIAL RESULTS

2.3.1 ROOTS AND CULTURAL BACKGROUND OF COMPLIANCE IN THE US

The literature indicates a disagreement concerning the origins of Compliance. Five developments in different business sectors profoundly influenced the evolution of Compliance. In the US, it seems that the origins of Compliance go back to the healthcare sector, US export regulation, the Anglo-American banking world, the avoidance of criminal liability of corporations, and the prevention of anti-trust violations, *e.g.* "Electrical Cases" (Eufinger, 2012, p. 21). In conclusion, Compliance means different things to different business sectors. For the purpose of my thesis, it will examine the origins in the laws.

The literature acknowledges that the origins of corporate Compliance are a product of the Federal Securities Laws. However, Miller (2014, p. 2) stated that the early starting point might be the Interstate Commerce Act of 1887.[20] Other authors, such as Taylor (2006, p. 54) and Fanto (2013, p. 11), held that in the US the term *"Compliance"* refers to the need to comply with the 1930s Securities Laws. In response to the financial crisis, the collapse of the financial markets and the Depression of the 1930s, the US government enacted the Securities Acts of 1933[21], 1934,[22] and other regulatory provisions (Miller, 2014, p. 3). This is also emphasized by Taylor (2006, p. 54) and Fanto (2013, p. 11) in their discussion on the evolution of Compliance.

---

[20] In 1887, Congress passed the Interstate Commerce Act, making the railroads the first industry subject to Federal regulation. The Act addressed the problem of railroad monopolies by setting guidelines for how the railroads could do business. This Act was the first federal law to regulate private industry in the United States. *See*, available at http://www.ourdocuments.gov/doc.php?flash=true&doc=49, (accessed: 28 March 2015).

[21] Enacted May 27, 1933, codified at 15 USC. § 77a et seq.

[22] Enacted June 6, 1934, codified at 15 USC. § 78a et seq.

2.3.1.1 Definitions of Compliance in the United States

To address the roots of Compliance in America, the term Compliance has to be described. Additionally, the term Compliance has to be distinguished from the term *"Ethics"* because in North America these two issues have often been combined.

More specifically with regard to business, the business ethics literature often describes Compliance as *"adherence with all the laws, regulations, rules, and policies governing an organization"* (Gnazzo, 2011, p. 538). Therefore, Compliance focuses on observing and monitoring the existing provisions, rules and guidelines. In contrast, Ethics is defined as a core *"set of beliefs and principles"* (Joyner & Payne, 2002, p. 299). In this context, Ethics is more than Compliance. The purpose of business ethics is "*to improve the ethical quality of decision making and acting at all levels of business*" (Enderle, 1996, pp. 37-38). Ethics and Compliance together require that the employees have to act in accordance with their legal, regulatory and professional obligations (Fanto, 2013, p. 11).

To summarize all these definitions in the field of business ethics in North America: Compliance is a concept of what is right and fair conduct or behavior or, in other words*: "an act of conforming or complying".*[23] In the broad sense, therefore, Compliance is a concept of behaviour.

2.3.1.2 The Historical Evolution of the American Compliance Function

To answer the research questions, it is furthermore necessary to refer to the legal requirements when appointing a Compliance Officer. The Compliance function was first established in the securities industry in the early 1960s (Baer, 2014, p. 142; Baker, et al., 2005, p. 5). Before this time, responsibility for Compliance functions was incumbent upon legal departments (Baker, et al., 2005, p. 5). This function focuses on the task of ensuring Compliance with legal and ethical norms from the inside out. The position should therefore be

---

[23] *See*, available at: http://www.webster-dictionary.org/definition/Compliance, (accessed: 28 March 2015).

a combination of Compliance detection, prevention, and response policies (DeStefano, 2013, p. 93).

In the securities industry and securities firms, the role of the Chief Compliance Officer is clearly defined and distinguished from business duties (Baker, et al., 2013, p. 6). For instance, the objective of the Compliance function is to advise businesses on how to comply with applicable laws and regulations (Baker, et al., 2005, p. 5). Compliance personnel should be solely responsible for monitoring business activity and employee conduct, in order to identify violations of rules, regulations, policies, and procedures (Baker, et al., 2013, p. 6).

Starting with the Exchange Act of 1934, the Securities and Exchange Commission (SEC)[24] was empowered with broad authority over all aspects of the securities industry.[25] A clear emphasis on the importance of Compliance was that a broker-dealer and its employees must conduct their business in accordance with their legal, regulatory, and professional obligations (Fanto, 2013, p. 11). However, Section 15 (b) (4) (D) allowed the SEC to discipline only the firm, not the violating employee. This problem was resolved by adding Sections 15 (b) (4) (E) and 15 (b) (6) with the Amendments to the Act of 1964. Under Section 15 (b) (4) (E), a broker-dealer or an *"associated person"*[26] can be a subject to sanctions (Fanto, 2013, p. 12). Since these additional provisions came into force, the need for a firm function (*i.e.*, Compliance) has been reinforced and Compliance has been afforded strong enforcement opportunities (Fanto, 2013, p. 13). In sum, the SEC required a firm to have a Compliance department and a Compliance Officer. In turn, this approach became a model for other firms (Fanto, 2013, p. 15).

---

[24] The Securities and Exchange Commission has five Commissioners who are appointed by the President of the United States with the advice and consent of the Senate. The mission of the SEC is to protect investors, to maintain fair, orderly, and efficient markets, and facilitate capital formation, *See* available at http://www.sec.gov/about/whatwedo.shtml, (accessed: 28 March 2015), The term "Commission" also means the Securities and Exchange Commission as well.

[25] *See*, available at http://www.sec.gov/about/laws.shtml#secexact1934, (accessed: 28 March 2015).

[26] *See* 15 USC. § 78o – Sec. 15 (b) (6) an "Associated person" is defined as anyone "who, among other things, *willfully aids and abets a violation of the federal securities laws or who commits a supervisory violation."*; *See* also in Sec. 3 (a) (18) *"any partner, officer, director, or branch manager of such broker or dealer (or any person occupying a similar status or performing similar functions), etc...."*.

Another milestone in advancing corporate Compliance was the promulgation by the US government of the Federal Sentencing Guidelines for Organizations (FSGO)[27] in 1991. The FSGO contains the first criminal justice framework for an effective corporate Compliance program. The FSGO outlines seven elements of effectiveness. These standards serve as a guide for the directors to ensure that reasonable Compliance is effectively established within their firms (Greenberg, 2010, p. 18). Therefore, the government has created more liability risk for directors. The 2004 amendments imposed responsibility for the Compliance program on an organization's *"governing authority"* or *"high-level personnel"*[28] (Greenberg, 2010, p. 35).

Since 1991, Corporate Compliance programs have become more prevalent on the whole in the US due to the influence of the FSGO. Meanwhile, several high-profile corporate cases brought under the FSGO prosecuted companies such as Archer Daniels Midland, Daiwa Bank, and Hoffman-La Roche (Greenberg, 2012, p. 7). Under the amendments of the US Federal Sentencing Guidelines of November 2004[29], private sector organizations are obliged to implement an effective Compliance program. The Compliance officer is an element of the Compliance organization. Hence, the position consists of efforts by organizations to ensure that employees do not violate applicable law (Miller, 2014, p. 1).

Today, in the so-called *"post-SOX era"*, best practice suggests that the role of a *"designated high-level official"* has come due to Sarbanes-Oxley Act of 2002 (SOX)[30], signed into law on July 30, 2002 as well as a number of other regulatory policies. The SOX 2002 was proposed to establish *"significantly higher standards for corporate responsibility and governance"*[31] to protect investors.

---

[27] The 1991 Guidelines Manual (effective November 1, 1991) – The current version of the FSGO can be found at: http://www.ussc.gov/guidelines-manual/1991/1991-federal-sentencing-guidelines-manual (accessed: 28 March 2015).

[28] U.S.S.C §8 B2.1.b (2) B (2004) *"High-level personnel of the organization shall ensure that the organization has an effective Compliance and ethics program, as described in this guideline. Specific individual(s) within high-level personnel shall be assigned overall responsibility for the Compliance and ethics program."*

[29] U.S.S.C §8 B2.1 (2004).

[30] The Sarbanes-Oxley Act of 2002 is Federal Law and mandatory. All listed organizations must comply. The legislation was enacted in 2002 and introduced major changes to the regulation of financial practice and corporate governance, available under: http://www.soxlaw.com/ (accessed: 28 March 2015).

[31] United States Congress, (2002). Senator Sarbanes, 148 Cong. Rec. S7350-04 in: Ethics Resource Center, 2007, p. 5.

This Act responded to questions concerning the role of corporate officers and imposed new legal duties upon them (Jones, 2007, p. 476). Since then, all listed companies in the US[32] have been affected by this Act (Shirley, 2004, p. 511).

In summary, it can be noted that in the US the first origin for laws related to Corporate Compliance programs appeared with the establishment of the FSGO in 1991. This was the legal starting point for companies to develop such programs (Greenberg, 2012, p. 7). In this context, Compliance and the Compliance Officer function in the US developed historically from self-regulatory attempts of corporations and the emergence of the FSGO to establish these standards with the force of law.

2.3.2 ROOTS AND CULTURAL BACKGROUND OF COMPLIANCE IN THE UK

Since the introduction of the Financial Services Bill in 1986,[33] Compliance has undergone a process of continual evolution in the United Kingdom. This was the beginning of the transformation from a self-regulated system to a statutory-based system. With this new legislation, the Financial Services firms began to realize that the term Compliance had gained a new significance and would have an important impact upon their operations (Taylor, 2006, p. 54). Until then, Compliance had almost been regarded as a "dirty word." However, since the enactment of this Act, Compliance has been recognized as an essential requirement of business duties (Edwards & Wolfe, 2005, p. 52).

---

[32] More than 1300 foreign corporations are listed in the US in: Shirley, 2004, p. 511.
[33] Proceeded through Parliament in 1985, enacted in 1986, came into force in 1988 as the Financial Services Act, *See*, available at: http://www.legislation.gov.uk/ukpga/1986/60/contents, (accessed: 28 April 2015).

In 2000 the Financial Services Authority (FSA)[34], has been formed as a unitary regulator on principles-based financial services regulation. The FSA was granted its statutory powers by the Financial Services and Markets Act 2000 (FSMA).[35] This supervisor moved to a principles-based regime in 2003 (Ford, 2008, p. 1) and regulated the majority of financial services markets, exchanges and firms. It set the standards and could take action against firms that failed to meet the required standards.[36] This marked the definitive end of self-regulation, and the advent of statutory regulations in the UK (Taylor, 2006, p. 55).

Furthermore, the increasing importance and significance of Compliance in the UK came to the fore in the banking industry for two reasons. First, from 2007 the Basel Capital Accord (Basel II) has required banks to manage all their risks through effective internal risk management procedures. Secondly, there has also been a major focus of attention in light of a number of high profile bankruptcies in the corporate sector (Edwards & Wolfe, 2004, p. 217).

Nevertheless, it was not only in the financial service sector that the significance of Compliance was on the rise. Arcot, et al. (2009), analyzed a database of 245 non-financial services companies for the period 1998-2004. They found that the Combined Code[37] fostered Compliance in the private sector (2009, p. 2). This Code linked and improved the two previous codes: Cadbury 1992[38] and Greenbury 1995.[39] The Cadbury Report was the UK response to the corporate scandals, *e.g.* Maxwell Communications. This report made a number of important recommendations relating to internal monitoring mechanisms in UK public limited companies. The objective was to improve the quality of monitoring by means of

---

[34] Financial Services Authority - was a supervisor oft he financial market, given statutory powers by the Financial Services and Markets Act 2000 in the United Kingdom between 2001 and 2013, *See* available at: http://www.fsa.gov.uk/about/who, (accessed: 28 April 2015).

[35] Financial Services and Markets Act (2000), Chapter 8, Part I, Sec. 1 The Regulator – "*The body corporate known as the Financial Services Authority The Financial ("the Authority") is to have the functions conferred on it by or under this Act*" *See*, available at: http://www.legislation.gov.uk/ukpga/2000/8/contents, (accessed: 28 April 2015). The Act was enacted on June 14, 2000.

[36] *See, Supra,* footnote 30.

[37] UK Combined Code of Corporate Governance ("the Code"), published in June 1998.

[38] Published in December 1992, the Financial Aspects of Corporate Governance - see available under: http://www.ecgi.org/codes/documents/cadbury.pdf, (accessed: 28 April 2015) – the objectives of the code are focused on the control and reporting functions of boards, and on the role of auditors. The Committee's recommendation is a Code of Best Practice designed to achieve the necessary high standards of corporate behavior.

[39] Code of Best Practice in determining and accounting for Directors' remuneration.

a Code of Practice. The firms were expected to adopt the Code recommendations relating to monitoring procedures (Weir & Laing, 2000, p. 279).

Thus, it can be seen that the UK has adopted a new and flexible approach known as "Comply or Explain." This approach is characterized by voluntary Compliance with the recommended provisions, and mandatory disclosure (Arcot, et al., 2009, pp. 4-5). Although the Code is voluntary, the London Stock Exchange requires listed firms to explain their governance policies and to give reasons for failure to comply with it. In the view of Weir & Laing (2000,) this public justification may explain the considerable growth in Compliance in the UK (p. 279).

Overall, UK Compliance was developed largely by the Financial Services and Markets Act 2000 and as an effective monitoring mechanism within companies. In contrast to the mandatory system of the Sarbanes-Oxley Act in the US, the UK Combined Code of Corporate Governance flexibly allows firms to choose whether to comply with its principles or to explain why they do not (Arcot, et al., 2009, p. 2).

2.3.2.1 THE DEFINITION OF COMPLIANCE IN THE UNITED KINGDOM

According to the American definition the British literature describes the general term of Compliance as "... *the adherence by the regulated to rules and regulations laid down by those in authority"* (Edwards & Wolfe, 2005, p. 48). However, in a broader sense, Compliance links to other aspects of duties. The term also includes concepts of obedience, observance, deference, governability... etc. Compliance has links to both business and the consumer and was established in the financial services sector. The investment businesses (*e.g.* banks, insurance companies, building societies and others) have to comply with the conduct and business requirements set out by the FSA (Edwards & Wolfe, 2006). In the view of Parker (2002, p.22), defining corporate Compliance is a difficult task. She emphasizes that *"regulatory Compliance"* could be defined as obedience to the law (Parker, 2002, p. 22). She assumed that Compliance implies a simplistic obedience to rules, rather than engagement with ethical and social responsibilities (Parker, 2002, p. 27). In her interpretation, the term Compliance is too restrictive. Compliance should be involved with its legal, social, environmental and ethical responsibilities and understood as a model of Compliance or a Compliance program (Parker, 2002, p. 27).

In conclusion, the United Kingdom definition of Compliance contains more than the American description. The enviroment is included and combined with the broader meaning of this term, e.g. ethical behaviour, group and individual responsibility, open relationship with the regulator, and ...etc. One reason for this might be the distinction from Compliance and Ethics.[40]

2.3.2.2 THE HISTORICAL EVOLUTION OF THE COMPLIANCE FUNCTION IN THE UK

While many authors might agree that Compliance relates to financial services legislation, the UK does not have any official definition of Compliance Officer. Compliance in the financial service sector as a function has evolved over the last 30 years within the UK. Since the introduction of the most important legislation, the Financial Services Act 1986, the senior management of the Financial Services firms have identified executives to review these provisions. These executives have not always been called Compliance Officers (Taylor, 2006, p. 54). Only in recent years have Compliance Officers with a professional background been selected and have come to be seen as "experts" (Taylor, 2006, p. 55).

In addition, a consultative document from the Basel Committee on Banking Supervision further supported this development. In April 2005, the Basel Committee on Banking Supervision[41] published ten principles for the Compliance function in banks. The paper defines this function as *"An independent function that identifies, assesses, advises on, monitors, and reports on the bank's Compliance risk, [...] to comply with all applicable laws, regulations, and codes of conduct and standards of good practice."*[42] Two principles of the Compliance function were emphasized: First, the role and responsibilities should be clearly identified, and second, the function should be independent from the business activities of the bank (Basel Committee on Banking Supervision, 2005, pp. 9-10; Edwards & Wolfe, 2004).

---

[40] *See supra* p. 51.
[41] Basel Committee on Banking Supervision (2005), *See* available at: http://www.bis.org/publ/bcbs113.pdf (accessed: 28 April 2015).
[42] *Ibid.*, Para. 10, p. 3.

As previously discussed,[43] outside the banking sector the new UK legislation and the increasing responsibilities of the corporate management have combined the practice of business with social and legal requirements and have strongly supported the transformation of the position of Compliance manager into a self-regulatory function within UK companies (Parker, 2002, p. 168). Parker (2002, p. 168) argued about the two faces of the Compliance role. In her view, this function contains a harmonizing and a political, conflict-handling role, which cannot be separated from one another. However, the UK Compliance function should be involved in the interests of developing the most conducive Compliance culture within organizations.

2.3.3 ROOTS AND CULTURAL BACKGROUND OF COMPLIANCE IN GERMANY

In Germany, the term Compliance is relatively new and has only been discussed for about ten years (Vetter, 2009, p. 33). In 2008, a German listed company in the US, Siemens AG, was allegedly involved in bribery. The organization was involved in more than US$ 1,4 billion in bribes to foreign officials in various countries. Siemens ultimately agreed to pay US$ 800 million in fines and penalties (Siebler, 2014, p. 3; Köhler, 2012, p. 612). Since then, Siemens has undergone a complete Compliance transformation and Compliance has entered the public arena in Germany. The enforcement of Compliance through the accelerating globalization of economic transactions, growing economic pressure, and increasing complex international legal norms and regulations also led to the need for human values and patterns of behavior within German companies (Palazzo, 2002, p. 195). In her view, German companies are very reluctant to address normative questions publicly. However, like many other trends, Compliance issues came from the US to Europe and Germany (Palazzo, 2002, p. 196). In accordance with the strict legislation in force there, American companies have developed a very explicit way of dealing with the norms and have introduced so-called "Compliance programs." Due to the different cultural backgrounds between the

---

[43] See supra p. 54.

US and Germany, many US companies have implemented formal business Compliance programs in their German branches and subsidiaries (Palazzo, 2002, p. 195).

Therefore, the concept of Compliance does not relate to any German historical roots. Viewed from a historic perspective, the concept of Compliance has been transferred from the US to Germany (Siebler, 2014, p. 4). On the assumption that German firms need to remain competitive internationally, they should have to comply with increasing requirements of adherence with legal provisions. Particularly with regard to the pressure on listed German companies in the US under the Sarbanes-Oxley Act 2002 and the regulations set forth with the US Securities and Exchange Commission (SEC), the concept has been adopted in Germany (Meier, 2011, p. 779).

2.3.3.1 THE DEFINITION OF COMPLIANCE IN GERMANY

According to many German authors,[44] the term Compliance originated from the Anglo-American legal terminology. The word Compliance has been adopted into German legal terminology without translation. It constitutes a so-called *"legal transplant"* (Groß, 2012, p. 34). The word represents a generic term with its origins in the English verb *"to comply with"* (Siebler, 2014, p. 3). Translated literally, Compliance means *"einhalten"* or *"befolgen"*. In fact, at first it describes a fundamental implicitness: The organization and each employee have always acted in Compliance with applicable laws. Therefore, Compliance has been described in the strictest sense of the word (Achenbach & Ransiek, 2012, p. 47). Then, the second element of Compliance requires an organizational model with processes and structures capable of ensuring adherence with corporate policies. (Gösswein & Hohmann, 2011, p. 963).

---

[44] *See, e.g.,* Eufinger, 2012; Gösswein & Hohmann, 2011; Groß, 2012; Siebler, 2014.

In conformity with the American and UK roots of legal definitions in the Securities Laws, it is not surprising that the first German codification was enacted in the Banking Act[45] and Securities Trading Act.[46] Under these provisions,[47] service enterprises must have a properly established internal business organization guaranteeing the adherence of the legal provision. From the financial services sector and through legislation, the term has become embedded in private sector organizations.

Apart from these specific sectoral rules and norms, there is no general legal definition of Compliance in Germany. According to no. 4.1.3., of the German Corporate Governance Code (DCGK)[48] the word Compliance is described as follows *"The Management Board ensures that all provisions of law and the enterprise's internal policies are abided by and works to achieve Compliance therewith by group companies (Compliance)."*[49] Thus, since 2007, a definition of Compliance has been included in the Code (Hauschka, 2010, p. 629). This general description of the term serves to determine the definition with regard to listed corporations (Vetter, 2009, p. 33). The German Corporate Governance Code formulates recommendations for self-imposed obligations of the companies concerned and does not have any legal force (Gösswein & Hohmann, 2011, p. 964). The German listed companies on DAX and MDAX are required to publish a declaration of conformity according to Section 161 German Stock Corporation Act.[50] Similar to the "Comply or Explain" approach in the UK, the executive board of the listed company issued an annual declaration to the effect that the recommendations of the "Deutscher Corporate Governance Kodex" have been, and are being complied with, or which of the Code's recommendations are not being applied, and why.

---

[45] Gesetz über das Kreditwesen, *See*, available under: http://www.gesetze-im-internet.de/kredwg/ (accessed: 25 May 2015).
[46] Gesetz über den Wertpapierhandel, *See*, available under: http://www.gesetze-im-internet.de/wphg/ (accessed: 25 May 2015).
[47] German Banking Act, § 25a (1934, 2007 Implementation of the Markets in Financial Instruments Directive (2006/73/EU); Securities Trading Act, § 33 (1994; last amendment BGBl. I p. 434, 566).
[48] The German Corporate Governance Code, (DCGK) as amended on November 7, 2002, effective until July 3, 2003) presents essential statutory regulations for the management and supervision of German listed companies and contains, in the form of recommendations and suggestions, internationally and nationally acknowledged standards for good and responsible corporate governance. *See*, available at: http://www.dcgk.de/en/, (accessed: 25 May 2015).
[49] German Corporate Governance Code, DCGK (2002), as amended on June 14, (2007).
[50] Stock Corporation Act (1937), *See*, available at: http://www.gesetze-im-internet.de/aktg/, (accessed: 25 May 2015).

In summary, the focus on the German definition of Compliance is derived from legal requirements of the financial services sector. In Germany, Compliance means not only adherence to the letter of the law, but is also just as concerned with obedience, observance, deference to the spirit of the law and the concepts set down in the DCGK.

2.3.3.2 THE HISTORICAL EVOLUTION OF THE GERMAN COMPLIANCE FUNCTION

In Germany, the legal roots of the Compliance function were laid in terms of *"Compliance rules"*[51] within the financial service sector in 1999. This directive provided for the establishment of a Compliance function. Under no. 4.1., the executive board of the service enterprises may set up a Compliance position to monitor the organizational duties.[52] This function should operate independently from the other business units and reports directly to the executive management.[53] It is interesting to note in this context that the German Compliance function was previously mentioned only in the form of the word 'Compliance'.

A further step toward establishing a Compliance function in the banking industry was taken in the form of the Basel Capital Accord (Basel II) since 2007. Pursuant to this, the banks have to manage all their risks through an effective internal risk management procedure. The minimal requirements for the legal position are set by the German Federal Financial Supervisory Authority[54] in the MAComp.[55] In this letter, the Compliance Officer's independence and assurance of prohibition of discrimination should be promoted by appointment for a 24-month period and a 12-month notice period for termination of the employment contract.

---

[51] Richtlinie des Bundesaufsichtsamtes für den Wertpapierhandel zur Konkretisierung der Organisationspflichten von Wertpapierdienstleistungsunternehmen gemäß § 33 Abs. 1 WpHG vom 25. Oktober 1999, *See*, available at: http://www.uni-leipzig.de/bankinstitut/files/dokumente/1999-10-25-01_0.pdf, (accessed: 25 May 2015).
[52] Ibid, Sec. 4, no. 4.1
[53] Ibid, Sec. 4, no. 4.2
[54] Federal Financial Supervisory Authority (BaFin) - This is an autonomous public-law institution subject to the legal and technical supervision of the Federal Ministry of Finance. *See*, available at: http://www.bafin.de/EN/BaFin/bafin_node.html, (accessed: 25 May 2015).
[55] Minimal Requirements for Compliance.

Given the historical background[56] of Compliance, it is easy to understand the development of a separate organizational unit for Compliance in German organizations. Legal entities confronted with international competition and the legislation have to take measures to comply with the legislative regulations and internal guidelines (Hauschka, 2010, p. 630). The Compliance Officer should be responsible for fulfilment of these requirements (Meier, 2011, p. 779). The challenge for the future will be how best to strengthen and structure this position.

---

[56] See supra p. 59.

2.4 CONCLUSION

Based on the literature analysis, it can be concluded that in the US, UK and in Germany, the roots of Compliance lie in the Securities Laws, with their stringent requirements in terms of adherence to the applicable rules and regulations. Nevertheless, on the other hand, the UK and Germany do not have any cultural background of Compliance. In the US, meanwhile, the first origins of Compliance go back to the 18th century, but it is sometimes unclear in the literature when exactly was the starting point. The term Compliance, Compliance efforts and discussions of organizational ethical culture have a longstanding tradition in the US. For more than a century, the boards and management of American companies have had to give due consideration to how best to prevent and detect corporate crime and misconduct. Since the birth of the FSGO, they have to continue to fill the gaps. As a result, of these developments, the US tended to develop a legal description of corporate Compliance and the corporate Compliance Officer.

Reviewing the literature, there is wide-ranging agreement that the Compliance function is a legal requirement. For example, the Compliance function in the financial sector originated from the Securities Laws in the US and the Financial Services Bill in the UK (Taylor, 2006, p. 54). In Germany, there is a commitment to establish a Compliance position in securities-related services enterprises under § 33 para 1 no. 1 German Securities Trading Act. As for legal characteristics of the German Compliance Officer, these are provided only for organizations that operate in heavily regulated industries such as financial services.

Finally, the first findings of the historical legal origins of the Compliance function are presented in a brief tabular overview in *table 1* below:

	US		UK		Germany	
	Compliance	CO	Compliance	CO	Compliance	CO
Origins	Railroads (1887)	Watergate Scandal	Since new legislation (1986)		No origins	
Cultural background	Ethics issues due to Protestantism		Self-regulated system, Importation of American Corporate Compliance.		No background, Importation of American Corporate Compliance	
Legal roots in the financial service sector	Federal Sec. Law		Fin. Service Bill	Basel II	Banking Act	Basel II
Legal roots in the private sector	Since 1991 by FSGO, SOX 2002	Since 2004 by FSGO	UKBA 2010 § 7 (2)	Not yet	No origin	Not yet
Legal definition in the private sector	U.S.S.C §8 B2.1 (2004)	U.S.S.C §8 B2.1. (b) (2)(B) (2004)	(Comb. Code)	Not yet	DCGK (2002)	Not yet
Approach	mitigating fact, SOX mandatory		Comply or Explain		Comply or Explain	
Department	Legal or Compliance Department		Usu. Compliance Department		Usu. Compliance Department	
Role	risk-management	dual-hatted	risk-management	two faces	risk-management	?

Table 1: Compliance Function Matrix – Historical Legal Origins (State of Research in 2014)

In conclusion, the American development and description of Compliance and the function of the Compliance Officer was supported by legislation. The legislation and the creation of regulators grew from the importance of the financial services sector in the US and the UK, the global financial crisis, and numerous corporate scandals. As for the development in the US, it might be said that the American system features a legal definition of Compliance and the position of the Compliance Officer. Since the birth of the FSGO in 1991, the US has begun to continue to fill the legal gap. The more recent American legislation greatly influenced global trade. Hence, the European organizations and companies are involved.

REFERENCES

Achenbach, H. & Ransiek, A., 2012. *Handbuch Wirtschaftsstrafrecht.* 3. ed. Heidelberg: C.F.Müller.

Arcot, S., Bruno, V. & Faure-Grimaud, A., 2009. Corporate Governance in the UK: Is the Comply or Explain Approach Working?. pp. 1-31.

Baer, M. H., 2014. Confronting the Two Faces of Corporate Fraud. *Florida Law Review*, April, 66 (Research Paper No. 377), pp. 87-155.

Baker, G., Castro, J. & Martin, L., 2005. The role of Compliance. *Journal of Investment Compliance*, 6(3), pp. 4-22.

Baker, G., Cavness, P. & Jones, E., 2013. [Online] Available at: http://www.goodriskgovernancepays.com/SIFMA-evolving-role-of-Compliance-2013.pdf [Accessed 21 March 2015].

Basel Committee on Banking Supervision, 2005. *http://www.bis.org/publ/bcbs113.pdf.* [Online] Available at: http://www.bis.org/publ/bcbs113.pdf [Accessed 28 04 2015].

Bernstein, S., Kelly, M. & Coy, K., 2012. *State of Compliance: 2012 Study,* s.l.: PwC and Compliance Week.

Campos Nave, J. A., 2009. *Strafbarkeit des Compliance Officer aufgrund einer aus dem Aufgabenbereich abgeleiteten Garantenstellung,* www.betriebs-berater.de: Betriebs-Berater.

Chew, P. K., 1997. *Directors' and Officers' Liability.* 4. Hrsg. New York: Practising Law Institute.

Consero Group LLC., 2012. *www.consero.com.* [Online] Available at: http://consero.com/2012-chief-Compliance-officer-data-survey/ [Accessed 20 April 2015].

DeMott, D. A., 2013. The Crucial but (Potentially) Precarious Position of the Chief Compliance Officer. *Brooklyn Journal of Coporate, Financial & Commercial Law,* 8(1), pp. 56-79.

DeStefano, M., 2013. Creating a Culture of Compliance: Why Departmentalization May Not Be the Answer. *Hastings Business Law Journal,* pp. 71-182.

Djilani, J. N., 2010. The British Importation of American Corporate Compliance. *Brooklyn Law Review,* 76(1), pp. 303-341.

Edwards, J. & Wolfe, S., 2004. The Compliance function in banks. *Journal of Financial Regulation and Compliance,* 12(3), pp. 216-227.

Edwards, J. & Wolfe, S., 2005. Compliance: A review. *Journal of Financial Regulation and Compliance,* 13(1), p. 48–59.

Edwards, J. & Wolfe, S., 2006. A Compliance competence partnership approach model. *Journal of Financial Regulation and Compliance*, 14(2), pp. 140-150.

Enderle, G., 1996. FOCUS: A Comparison of Business Ethics in North America and Continental Europe. *Business Ethics A European Review*, 5(1), pp. 33-46.

Ethics Resource Center, 2007. *Ethics Resource Center.* [Online] Available at: www.ethics.org/CECO Accessed 15 March 2015].

Eufinger, A., 2012. Zu den historischen Ursprüngen der Compliance. *CCZ*, pp. 21-24.

Fanto, J. A., 2013. Surveillant and Counselor: A Reorientation in Compliance for Financial Firms. *Brooklyn Law School*, Working Paper Series(Research Paper No. 358), pp. 1-65.

Ford, C. L., 2008. New Governance, Compliance, and Principles-Based Securities Regulation. *American Business Law Journal*, 45(1), pp. 1-60.

Freeman, E. H., 2007. Regulatory Compliance and the Chief Compliance Officer. *Information Security Journal*, 19 Dec., 16(6), pp. 357-361.

Geiger, D., 2011. Nemo ultra posse obligatur - Zur strafrechtlichen Haftung von Compliance-Beauftragten ohne Disziplinargewalt. *CCZ*, pp. 170-174.

Gläser, J. & Laudel, G., 2010. *Expterteninerviews und qualitative Inhaltsanalyse.* 4. ed. Wiesbaden: VS Verlag für Sozialwissenschaft | Springer Fachmedien.

Gnazzo, P. J., 2011. The Chief Ethics and Compliance Officer: A Test of Endurance. *Business and Society Review*, Issue 4, p. 533–553.

Gösswein, G. & Hohmann, O., 2011. *Betriebs-Berater*, April, Volume 16, pp. 963-968.

Greenberg, M. D., 2009. *Perspectives of Chief Ethics and Compliance Officers on the Detection and Prevention of Corporate Misdeeds.* Santa Monica, RAND Corporation.

Greenberg, M. D., 2010. *Directors as Guardians of Compliance and Ethics Within the Corporate Citadel.* Santa Monica, Calif., RAND Corporation.

Greenberg, M. D., 2012. *Corporate Culture and Ethical Leadership Under the Federal Sentencing Guidelines.* Santa Monica, RAND Corporation, Center for Corporate Ethics and Governance.

Greenberg, M. D., 2014. *Transforming Compliance: Emerging Paradigms for Boards, Management, Compliance Officers, and Government.* Santa Monica, Calif., RAND Corporation.

Groß, N. F. V., 2012. *Chief Compliance Officer.* 1. ed. ugsburg: Nomos Verlag.

Hauschka, C. E., 2010. *Compliance als Teil einer modernen Unternehmensführung*, s.l.: AnwBl 2010.

Hauschka, C. E., 2014. Zum Berufsbild des Compliance Officers. *CCZ*, pp. 165-170.

Hoffman, W. M., Neill, J. D. & Stovall, O. S., 2008a. Mutual Fund Compliance Officer Independence and Corporate Governance. *Business and Society Review*, 16(1), pp. 52-60.

Hoffman, W. M., Neill, J. D. & Stovall, O. S., 2008b. An Investigation of Ethics Officer Independence. *Journal of Business Ethics*, Volume 78, p. 87–95.

Hopt, K. J., 2006. Comparative Company Law. In: M. P. I. f. C. a. I. P. Law, ed. *The Oxford Handbook of Comparative Law*. s.l.:s.n., pp. 1161-1191.

Jones, A. (2007). Corporate Officer Wrongdoing and the Fiduciary Duties of Corporate Officers under Delaware Law. *American Business Law Journal*, 44(3), pp. 475–520.

Joyner, B. E. & Payne, D., 2002. Evolution and Implementation: A Study of Values, Business Ethics and Corporate Social Responsibility. *Journal of Business Ethics*, Volume 41, p. 297–311.

Köhler, M., 2012. Revisiting a Foreign Corrupt Practice Act Compliance Defense. *Wisconsin Law Review*, pp. 609-659.

LLC, C. G., 2012. *2012 Chief Compliance Officer Data Survey,* Bethesda: Consero Group LLC.

Majewski, T. M., 2006. Conflicts of interest chief Compliance officers face in implementing Compliance programs for investment funds and investment advisers. *Journal of Investment Compliance*, 7(4), pp. 23-27.

Meaney, M. E., 2001. Professional Ethical Developmemt in Health Care Compliance. In: *Guide to Professional Development in Compliance*. Gaithersburg, Maryland: Aspen Publishers, Inc., pp. 1-18.

Meier, H.-G., 2011. Der Arbeitsvertrag des Compliance-Beauftragten – Rechtliche Notwendigkeiten und Möglichkeiten. *NZA*, pp. 779-782.

Michaels, R., 2005. *The Functional Method of Comparative Law,* Duke Law School: Oxford University Press.

Miller, G. P., 2014. The Compliance function: an overview. *LAW & ECONOMICS RESEARCH PAPER SERIES*, November, Volume WORKING PAPER NO. 14-36.

Palazzo, B., 2002. U.S.-American and German Business Ethics: An Intercultural Comparison. *Journal of Business Ethics*, 41(3), pp. 195-216.

Parker, C., 2000. The Ethics of Advising on Regulatory Compliance: Autonomy or Interdependence?. *Journal of Business Ethics*, Volume 28, p. 339–351.

Parker, C., 2002. *The Open Corporation.* 1. ed. Cambridge: Cambridge University Press.

Pirraglia, A., 2003. A Tangled Web: Compliance Director Liability Under the Securities Laws. *Fordham Journal of Corporate & Financial Law,* 8(1), pp. 245-272.

PWC, 2012. *PWC.* [Online] Available at: http://www.pwc.com/us/stateofCompliance [Accessed 20 April 2015].

PWC, 2014. *PWC.* [Online] Available at: http://www.com/us/stateofCompliance [Accessed 20 April 2015].

Raus, N. & Lützeler, M., 2012. Berichtspflicht des Compliance Officers – zwischen interner Eskalation und externer Anzeige. *CCZ,* pp. 96-101.

Renz, H. & Wybitul, T., 2012. Im Blickpunkt: Das Berufsbild des Compliance-Beauftragten Ein modernes Verständnis von Compliance. *Betriebs-Berater,* Issue 3, pp. VI-VII.

Rosella, M. R. & Pugliese, D., 2006. The investment company chief Compliance officer: three years later – an assessment of the evolution of the role of the CCO. *Joournal of Investment Compliance,* 7(4), pp. 16-22.

Rosen, R. E., Parker, C. E. & Lehmann Nielsen, V., 2013. *The Framing Effects of Professionalism: Is There a Lawyer Cast of Mind? Lessons From Compliance Programs,* Miami: s.n.

Shirley, J. (2004). International Law and the Ramifications of the Sarbanes-Oxley Act of 2002. *Boston College International and Comparative Law Review,* 27(2), pp. 501-528.

Siebler, B., 2014. *Criminal Compliance im interdisziplinären Kontext.* 1. ed. Hamburg: Diplomica-Verlag.

Taylor, C., 2006. The evolution of Compliance. *Journal of Investment Compliance,* 6(4), pp. 54-58.

The Committee on the Financial Aspects of Corporate Governance, 1992. http://www.ecgi.org/codes/documents/cadbury.pdf. [Online] Available at: http://www.ecgi.org/codes/documents/cadbury.pdf [Accessed 28 April 2015].

Traeger, H. & Jimbo, M., 2014b. Supervisory Liability: The SEC's Scrutiny and Support of Chief Compliance Officers: Part 2. *The Investment Lawyer,* pp. 12-21.

Traeger, H., Jimbo, M. & Guidroz, K. E., 2014a. Supervisory Liability: The SEC's Scrutiny and Support of Chief Compliance Officers: Part 1. *The Investment Lawyer,* pp. 25 - 35.

U.S. Sentencing Guidelines Manual, 2013. *2013 USSC GUIDELINES MANUAL,* Washington, DC: s.n.

Vetter, 2009. Compliance in der Unternehmenspraxis. In: G. Wecker & H. van Haak, eds. 2. ed. Wiesbaden: Springer Gabler.

Weber, J. & Fortun, D., 2005. Ethics and Compliance Officer Profile: Survey, Comparison and, Recommendations. *Business and Society Review*, 110(2), pp. 97-115.

Weir, C. & Laing, D., 2000. The Performance-Governance Relationship: The Effects of Cadbury Compliance on UK Quoted Companies. *Journal of Management and Governance*, Volume 4, p. 265–281.

Wolf, M., 2011. Der Compliance-Officer – Garant, hoheitlich Beauftragter oder Berater im Unternehmensinteresse Aufsichtsrecht?. *Betriebs-Berater*, Issue 22, pp. 1353-1360.

Zweigert, K. & Kötz, H., 1996. *Einführung in die Rechtsvergleichung*. 3. ed. Tübingen: Mohr Siebeck Verlag.

3
CRITICAL ANALYSIS OF THE PRECISION OF VALUATIONS IN FINANCIAL EXPERTS' FAIRNESS OPINIONS

Tobias Lippe

TABLE OF CONTENT
3.1 Introductory Case Study 73
3.2 Introduction 74
3.3 Fairness Opinions 77
3.4 Statistical Analysis 82
      3.4.1 Valuation Range 82
      3.4.2 Valuation Accuracy 84
3.5 Outlook 86
3.6 Conclusion 87
References 88

3.1 INTRODUCTORY CASE STUDY

In April 2010, the retailer group Talbots Inc. made a public offer to acquire the remaining stocks of BPW Acquisition Corp, a company already operating under the umbrella of Talbots Inc focussing on acquisitions and reorganisations within the group. Talbots Inc. was willing to offer USD 7.10 for each share of BPW. In order to foster the process, BPW's executive board hired Financo, a relatively small investment bank, as a financial advisor[1].

Financo applied discounted cash flow, market multiples depending on market capitalization to EBIT and comparable transaction multiples in its assessment of a fair market price for each BPW Acquisition stock. The resulting valuation estimates ranged from USD 7.16 to USD 15.20 for EBIT multiples, between USD 7.16 and USD 11.58 for comparable transaction multiples and USD 9.89 and USD 11.75 for the discounted cash flow valuation. As can be seen from the financial advisor's fairness opinion report, the already broad range of valuation estimates was beaten by a lower completion price.

---

[1] While auditors are forbidden to provide fairness opinions in the U.S. since the passage of the Sarbanes-Oxley Act, auditors are still free to render fairness opinions in most European countries.

3.2 INTRODUCTION

The importance of mergers and acquisitions (M&A) worldwide is large and sorely in the U.S. M&A activities total to a value of 1.95 trillion Dollars annually (Hahn, 2005). Due to the enormous size of the market nearly all medium and large banks are engaged to at least some extent in this area. Some banks do purely provide loans for mergers and acquisitions; others provide assistance or even carry out the deal. The fees paid for these services alone amounted to 5.5 billion Dollars between 1985 and 1993 or on average 0.85% of the deal's value (Servaes and Zenner, 1996).

Therefore, mergers and acquisitions are object of extensive attention, both from the academic area as well as popular or business oriented research. In the academic domain, corporate transactions are mostly examined from the perspective of agency theory, which is best described, according to Kroll et al. (2008), by the disconnection between managements' expectations (e.g. growth strategy) and shareholder's expectations (e.g. value creation).

Whereas managements' expectations and the later fulfilment of these drivers for M&A are hardly to be tested, the shareholder's returns can be measured precisely. Results are mixed, though.

Some results are positive, others negative or come to mixed results for different markets, variables or periods (Agrawal et al., 1992; Andrade et al., 2001; Asquith, 1983; Asquith and Kim, 1982; Jensen, 1986, Kroll et al., 1997). King et al. recapitulated these mixed results in their meta-analyses in 2004 in the way that the acquisition performance variance is linked to variables "yet to be identified" (King et al., 2004).

The role of investment banks in M&A has been covered by Servaes and Zenner (1996) and provided an answer to the question why investment banks are consulted in mergers and acquisitions although the costs for investment banks' advices are rather high. However, they find support for their hypothesis that the costs of getting advice of an investment bank can drop below the cost of asymmetric information costs.

Asymmetric information costs arise due to the complexity of transactions, complete takeovers versus the simple acquisition of some assets, the acquirer's experience in M&A and the diversification of the target (Servaes and Zenner, 1996). Servaes and Zenner found even evidence for a lower acquisition announcement return, if investment banks are involved.

The equation of asymmetric information costs and of returns is important in order to understand the role of fairness opinions in corporate transactions. Fairness opinions are generally sought to assist management in M&A and provide information that have been previously unavailable to management and external stakeholders (Essler et al., 2008 and Cain and Denis, 2010). Thus, fairness opinions help to overcome the costs of asymmetric information costs.

The costs for fairness opinions differ widely as well as the purpose they are requested. Some people believe that fairness opinions are mainly sought to protect management from litigation (Rau, 2000), others still assume a certain value underlying fairness opinions (Kisgen et al., 2008).

The introductory example of a fairness opinion provided by Financo already shows the problem of fairness opinions. Although the valuation rests on solid models like the discounted cash flow valuation, the conclusions drawn are rather weak. Besides a relatively large valuation range, the later paid price, either in cash or shares, does not need to be in this range. Hence, Cain and Denis (2010, p.7) insists that fairness opinions are just "rubber stamps".

Kisgen et al. were the first researches in 2008, who analysed different variables and the influence of those on the cumulative abnormal return of shares of companies using fairness opinions. Comparable to the normal research of cumulative abnormal returns carried out by researchers as Agrawal et al., (1992) and Jensen and Ruback (1983), a data set was chosen and the performance of the shares tested on the correlation with variables like size or industry relatedness.

Whereas research on cumulative abnormal returns of acquirers is interesting for potential and actual shareholders in these shares, the research does not answer the question why fairness opinions are not precise. Why do we sometimes see a valuation range of more than 100 per cent, but the later paid price is still outside that broad range?

Cain and Denis (2010) tackled the question whether fairness opinions contain useful information. Their first result that acquirer advisors derive on average a more optimistic valuation than the target's advisors seems to be plausible as acquirer's advisors should come up with an even more optimistic valuation than the offered premium, whereas target's advisors should reflect on a more pessimistic valuation in order to convince the respective shareholders.

The second result of Cain and Denis (2010) is new and of special interest for the thesis as it confirms that certain variables have an influence on the precision of fairness opinions, namely the reputation of financial advisors. Top-tier financial advisors create more precise valuations than lower-tier advisors. Furthermore, Cain and Denis were able to prove that contingency structures or contingency fees do not influence valuation accuracy. The reputation results will be tested again to underline the robustness of their findings and the current data set. The later results will be accepted as all mergers after 2002, who published fairness opinions, included at least the annotation that contingency fees might be paid.

Consequently, a legitimate question is why are fairness opinions so imprecise and what can be done to improve this? Should investors be more sensitive and consider fairness opinions just as an additional source of information in the long M&A process or is the valuation range positively or negatively correlated to certain variables?

Answering this question, the creators of fairness opinions might be able to deliver more precise valuations. On the other hand, the readers of fairness opinions are able to change their behaviour as well. Target and acquirer's management might be able to come to a fairer, so to say, better price and the target's shareholder will not sell their shares for an ill-advised price tag.

3.3 FAIRNESS OPINIONS

Although fairness opinions are used frequently in every major corporate control transaction like negotiated mergers, friendly or hostile tender offers, freeze-out mergers, self-tenders and leveraged buyouts, the introductory example of Talbots Inc. and BPW Acquisition Corp. has proven that fairness opinions cannot only be under- or overvaluing a target in mergers and acquisitions, it has also shown that even broad valuation ranges are not a guarantee for a later price lying in that range. This leads to the question how fair or useful fair-ness opinions are.

Therefore, researchers and even businesses have started to doubt the validity of fairness opinions. Some people, as Davidoff (2006), believe in fairness opinions only as a legal safeguard, which became a per-se requirement after the van-Gorkum ruling in 1985.

Bebchuk and Kahan (1989) distinguish the discretion in the term "fair from a financial point of view" as the main problem of fairness opinions and give an example of an undisclosed deal, where different definitions have led to fair estimations of $53, $80-85 and $91 per share, a valuation range of more than 70%.

Furthermore, both researchers raise the question, whether a formerly fair deal would become unfair, if another, higher, offer becomes available. In their mind set every offer below the highest offer must be unfair.

Antagonists of fairness opinions as Bebchuk and Kahan (1989) even assume that banks adapt fairness opinions to the wishes of managers as they are likely to be rehired when doing so, whereas opposing opinions will reduce the likelihood of getting rehired.

Others still believe in fairness opinions and assume at least a certain value in improving the transaction by providing information to shareholders, increasing the success rates of mergers, lower premiums or a better cumulative abnormal return. Perrone and Laird summarised the relevance of fairness opinions in 2002 by claiming fairness opinions might provide the company itself and its investors with a certain feeling of security of getting a fair deal as fairness opinions sometimes carve out deal breaking problems. However, these deal breaking problems are not explained.

Furthermore, fairness opinions can minimise the risk of disagreement between shareholders as well as the risk of litigation. In a similar vein, according to Servaes and Zenner (1996), investment banks reduce the information asymmetry between target firms and acquirers by issuing a fairness opinion.

Research results are mixed and provide no clear picture at the moment. However, even more fascinating, many people put affords in the way how fairness opinions are crafted. Regulators worldwide have set guidelines and rules how fairness opinions shall be provided. However, regulators did never investigate the reasons why fairness opinions do not provide a clear and precise valuation.

Despite their ubiquity, as the discussion has shown so far, fairness opinions are especially criticised by the legal community for their subjectivity, methodologically flawed analysis and the inherent conflicts of interest. Elson (1992, p. 1002) even concludes that fairness opinions are "as necessary to valuation analysis as is the appendix to the human digestive system" and that they produce no value for shareholders.

Especially in the 1980's, when fairness opinions become a common reference paper in mergers and acquisitions, researchers were at least sceptical towards fairness opinions.

By the end of the 1980's, Bebchuk and Kahan (1989) tried to investigate the reasons why fairness opinions are not as effective as they might be. Bebchuk and Kahan (1989) assume diverging valuation techniques in the valuation models as the key driver. Shaked and Kempainen (2009) state in the same vein the differences in the discounted cash flow valuation model that exist between business and theory.

In the 1990's the focus of investigation has shifted to mergers and acquisitions and the cumulative abnormal returns observable therein; but these papers ignored to measure the impact on fairness opinions. The paper of Servaes and Zenner in 1996, just to mention one out of many researches, consequently focusses on the role of certain partners or variables in mergers and acquisition, but do not link their results to fairness opinions.

Therefore, till the late 2000's, Bebchuk and Kahan (1989) delivered the best research asking how fair fairness opinions are and what can be done about it, but nevertheless they do not research the precision of fairness opinions. However, they argument theoretically some factors influencing fairness opinions like the objectivity of investment banks.

Davidoff took up the cudgels for fairness opinions in 2006 by summarising that the real information of fairness opinions is not the bottom-line conclusion, instead it is the valuation analysis. However, this information is said to be hard to find and often hidden by a stack of protective language to protect the investment bank from liability.

Kisgen et al. (2008) carried out a complex analysis of fairness opinions. They analyse the variables size, friendly or hostile, stock vs. cash payment, relatedness and corporate governance and their impacts on the deal completion, deal premium and announcement returns (CARs). By doing so, Kisgen et al. (2008) produced some helpful results that can be indirectly used for the measurement of precision in fairness opinions.

In 2010, Cain and Denis, carried out the first published research on the usefulness and precision of fairness opinion. Using a data set from 1998 to 2005, they were able to demonstrate a greater degree of valuation optimism for advisors working for acquirers than those working for targets as well as higher valuation accuracy for top-tier advisors compared to lower-tier advisors. Furthermore, the often discussed influence of contingency fees on the usefulness of fairness opinions was neglected as contingency fees are not related to the valuation accuracy. They conclude on the usefulness of opinions that they are informative if the valuation range is narrow, but uninformative when the range in valuations is great. Therefore, Cain and Denis imply a need for further research to narrow down the valuation range.

Since there is only the work of Cain and Denis (2010) on the key drivers of valuation precision in fairness opinions, who even put the scope of their research on a slightly different scale, my research will be of an exploratory nature. As the previous theoretical discussion has unfolded a bright range of variables and their influence on mergers and acquisitions in general, these variables will be used as a first indicator for a regression model.

Although these variables alone might not eliminate all uncertainty about the precision and usefulness of fairness opinions, it is likely that my research will reduce the valuation range and help shareholders to increase the benefits underlying every fairness opinion.

The following table summarises the variables and their perceived influence on the precision of fairness opinions, where a green arrow (upwards) indicates a good influence and, hence, a smaller valuation range or a higher accuracy. A yellow arrow (left to right) indicates an unclear direction of influence and a red arrow (downwards) a negative influence.

		same industry	
industry	↑	Servaes & Zenner (1996)	same industry more knowledge on discount rates
		payment options	
Stock	↓	Servaes & Zenner (1996)	more expertise is needed to sell securities
	↓	Kisgen et al. (2008)	valuations might fluctuate during transaction process
	↓	McLaughlin (1990)	higher premiums, higher risk
Cash	↑	Loughran and Vijh (1997)	CARs are better for M&A if cash is used
		Size of deal	
relative	↓	Kisgen et al. (2008)	impact on returns
	↓	Servaes & Zenner (1996)	more complex, more business units
absolute	↓	Kisgen et al. (2008)	higher risk for FO provider due to litigation,
	↑	Schwetzler & Aders (2008)	more FOs are used, all but one rely on business plans, which exist for large dea
	↑	Kisgen et al. (2008)	internal sources, assisting FO provider
	↑	Titman and Trueman (1986)	larger companies use better investment banks, which provide better services
		Reputation	
reputation	↑	Cain & Denis (2010)	proven to provide "significantly lower absolute estimation errors"
	↑	Kisgen et al. (2008)	lower deal premia, better calculation, lower tier focus on completion
	→	Rau (2000)	higher quality of M&A with more reputable advisors, but higher premiums are paid
	↓	Bebchuk & Kahan (1989)	top tier banks are used to certify
	→	Mikhail et al. (1998)	analyst turnover not linked to performance, only to relative precision
		FO requested by	
Acquirer	↓	Cain & Denis (2010)	and Cain & Denis (2012), mean range of 76% for acquirer, median 48%
Target	↑	Cain & Denis (2010)	and Cain & Denis (2012), mean range of 60% for acquirer, median 36%
		multiple advisors / multiple FO	
multiple advisor	↑	Shaked & Kampainen (2009)	lower premia, not lower estimation range
	→	Kisgen et al. (2008)	multiple advisors do not influence deal completion or premia, but multiple FO improve deal quality, more FO obtained in hostile deals
	↑	Bebchuk & Kahan (1989)	2 or more FO lower contingency problem, lower conflicts of interest

Illustration 1: variables for main research and their perceived direction of influence.

3.4 STATISTICAL ANALYSIS

Generally, two different measurements for precision are feasible.

A fairness opinion can be precise in the valuation range. A small valuation range is indicated by a small variance between the lower and upper value for every valuation model. However, a small valuation range does not imply a good valuation. It just indicates that both values are relatively next to each other. But both values might be wrong.

Consequently, the valuation accuracy is the second measurement. The accuracy can be measured by taking the values stated in the fairness opinion and putting them in contrast to the later paid price. On the other hand, an average accurate valuation can be obtained by two totally wrong valuations. The lower valuation comes to value of -70%, the higher valuation to +80%, the average would be +5%.

Therefore, both precision measurements should provide clear evidence for the independent variables in order to give a detailed and clear outcome what can be done to improve the precision, efficiency and finally the usefulness of fairness opinions.

3.4.1 VALUATION RANGE

The valuation range in fairness opinions is clearly smaller for non-financial mergers compared to financial mergers. Furthermore, top-tier investment banks offer smaller valuation ranges than top 20 investment banks and especially better ranges than the non-top 20 investment banks. For acquisitions with more than one fairness opinion the valuation range is, again, better. A previous relation between the company and the investment bank also helps to narrow down the valuation range. Additionally, larger deals by terms of market capitalisation (transaction volume) are also easier to value as the valuation range is smaller.

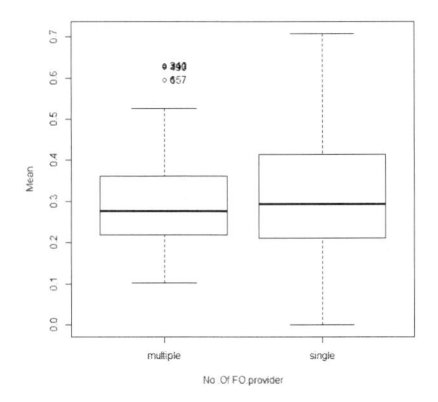

Illustration 2: valuation range for targets and acquirers depending on the number of fairness opinions per deal, source: own production

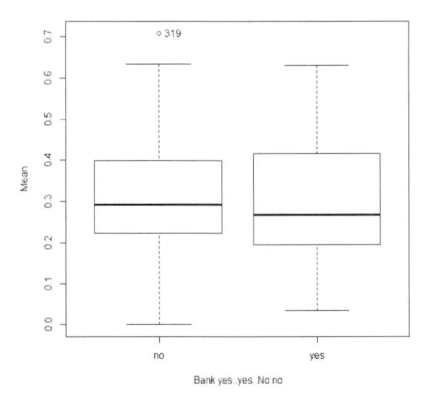

Illustration 3: valuation range for targets and acquirers depending on the dummy bank / non-bank, source: own production

These findings are also reliable and robust for individual tests for the targets and acquirers. Linear regression models for both, target and acquirers, have supported the importance and tendency of the independent variables to lower the valuation range.

3.4.2 VALUATION ACCURACY

The valuation accuracy allows to verify and transfer the findings to similar research as mentioned before. Cumulative abnormal returns (CARs) in mergers and acquisitions have shown that larger deals offer lower CARs as well as top-tier investment banks, just to mention a few (Rau, 2000, Cain and Denis, 2010). Cain and Denis (2010) have found an overvaluation in fairness opinions of +7% for acquirer's FO providers and an undervaluation of -15% by target's FO providers. Supporting the robustness of the used data sample, the tests of valuation accuracy support these findings.

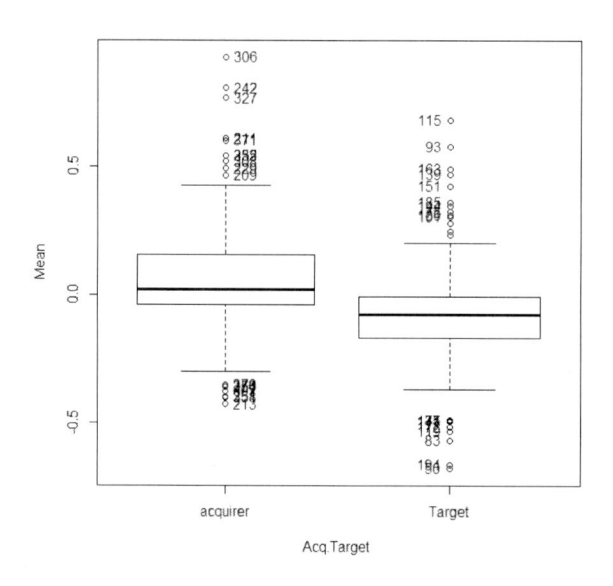

Illustration 4: valuation accuracy for targets and acquirers.

Fairness opinions crafted by the acquirer's bank overvalue the target by +4% on average, whereas the average mean valuation for the target issued by the target's investment bank is -8% to low. Hence, both fairness opinions support the fears of critical researchers towards fairness opinions as both results support the thesis of deal completion as the main goal for the issuer of fairness opinions. Target's shareholders are faced with a lower valuation indicating a good deal by accepting the acquisition, whereas the acquirer's shareholders are convinced by an overvaluation of the target. Overvaluation implies that a higher price would still be fair and the acquirer's management should close the deal before some else offers the higher price.

Further analysis support more precise valuations for non-bank mergers, in line with the argumentation found for the valuation range, higher ranked investment banks as well as the tendency of multiple fairness opinions to be more accurate.

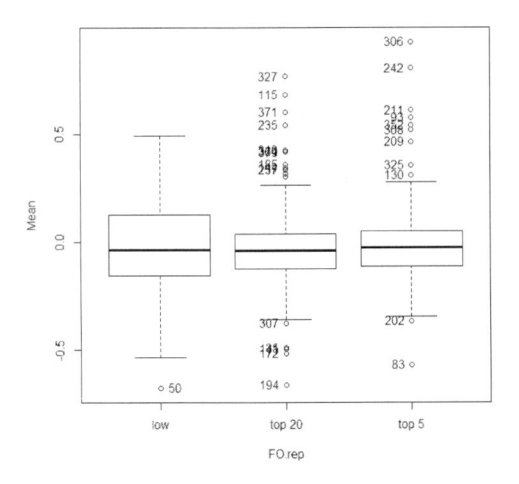

Illustration 5: valuation accuracy for targets and acquirers based on the reputation of fairness opinion's provider, source: own production.

At the current phase of research regression models as well as t-tests based on the accuracy for acquirers support the findings. The regression model shows a clear link between the mentioned independent variables and the mean accuracy of fairness opinions.

3.5 Outlook

Based on the findings so far, the regression analyses and t-tests have to be carried out for both precision measurements as well as for each sub-group. The distinction between targets and acquirers has proven to enhance the robustness of the results. Current results for the regression analyses have shown reliable results which are in line with expectations.

Furthermore, the data set consisting of mergers and acquisitions carried out between 2002 and 2013 offers the chance to evaluate different time periods. A first meaningful separation into three groups comes from the financial crisis which had its peak in 2008 and 2009. The precision might be lower in these years as comparable research on cumulative abnormal returns during the financial crises support such hypothesis. A separation into years from 2002 to 2007, 2008 and 2009 and 2010 to 2013 might support the hypothesis that the precision of fairness opinions is higher in years of relatively stable (financial) markets.

The second hypothesis is a separation into two samples based on changes in legislation. U.S. authorities have sharpened the rules for fairness opinion providers several times with the aim of increasing the usefulness and information content of fairness opinions.

The data set allows additionally to differentiate between the industry clusters targets belong to. Previous research has shown that some industries, comparable to the dummy variable bank/non-bank, offer higher valuation ranges than other industries. However, the data set does not contain enough differentiated mergers to further analyse cross-sectional premiums. Nonetheless, a differentiation might help to make some findings more robust.

3.6 CONCLUSION

Fairness opinions have been critically scrutinised for decades. However, research has not been able to come up with a common understanding on the usefulness of fairness opinions yet.

Nonetheless, fairness opinions have become a per-se requirement for mergers in the United States and, consequently, every effort should be taken to in-crease the value of every single fairness opinion.

By critics of fairness opinions, the per-se requirement is often described as a rubber stamp paper to protect management allowing them to foster unhealthy deals against the interests of shareholders. Thus, the first step was to prove a right to exist for fairness opinions and determining variables which might increase the underlying value of fairness opinions. Providing suitable variables for a data set of more than 300 mergers in the U.S. between 2002 and 2013 and the expected effects, beneficial or adverse, the paper already enhanced existing research.

The statistical analysis so far has shown that the precision of fairness opinions can be higher in certain situations. These situations are not always coincidentally reached. They could be changed by management or enforced with legislation as well. The first step was already taken in the U.S., where nowadays only investment banks are allowed to craft fairness opinions. If multiple fairness opinions or larger, more experienced investment banks help to enhance the quality of a fairness opinion, a mandatory push by legislation might be beneficiary for the precision and power of fairness opinions.

Finalising the statistical analysis will lead to a better understanding of fairness opinions and their precision. Readers of fairness opinions should be able to be more critical towards the content and used valuation models within fairness opinions and determine in how far the given valuation should be accepted. If shareholders are not convinced by the results they should be able to address management accordingly and ask for an improved, more precise opinion.

REFERENCES

Andrade, G., Mitchell, M. & Stafford, E. (2001) New evidence and perspectives on mergers. Journal of Economic Perspectives, 103-120.

Agrawal, A., Jeffrey P. J. & Gershon N. M. (1992) The post-merger performanceof acquiring firms: A re-examination of an anomaly, Journal of Finance 47, 1605-1622.

Asquith, P. (1983) Merger hids, uncertainty, and stockholder returns, Journal of Financial Economics 11, 51-83.

Asquith, P., Kim, E. H. (1982) The Impact of Merger Bids on the Participating Firms' Security Holders, The Journal of Finance 37, 1209-1228.

Bebchuck, L. A. & Kahan, M. (1998) Fairness Opinions: How Fair Are They and What Can be Done about it? Duke Law Journal, 27, 27-53.

Cain, M. D. & Denis, D. J. (2010) Do Fairness Opinion Valuations Contain Useful Information?.

Davidoff, S. M. (2006) Fairness Opnions. Wayne State University Law School Legal Studies Research Paper Series.

Elson, C. (1992) Fairnes Opinions: Are they fair or should we care? Ohio State Law Journal, 53, 951-970.

Essler, W., Lobe, S. & Röder, K., eds. (2008) Fairness Opinion: Grundlagen und Anwendung. Schäffer-Poeschel Verlag, Stuttgart.

Hahn, A. L. (2005), The Long Slode Stops For M&A Driven By A December Frenzy, U.S. Volume Climbs 46% in 2004, Investment Dealers Digest 17 January, p.1-2.

Jensen, M. C. (1986) Agency Cost Of Free Cash Flow, Corporate Finance, and Takeovers. American Economic Review, Vol. 76, No. 2, May 1986.

King, D. R., Dalton, D. R., Daily, C. M. and Covin, J. G. (2004), Meta-analyses of post-acquisition performance: indications of unidentified moderators. Strat. Mgmt. J., 25: 187–200.

Kisgen, D. J., Qian, J. & Song, W. (2008) Are Fairness Opinions Fair? The Case of Mergers and Acquisitions. Journal of Financial Economics, 91, 179-207.

Kroll, M., Walters, B. A. & Wright, P. (2008) Board vigilance, director experience, and corporate outcomes. Strategic Management Journal, 29, 363-382.

Loughran, T. & Vijh, A. M. (1997) Do long-term shareholders benefit from corporate acquisitions? Journal of Finance, 52, 1765-1790.

McLaughlin, R. (1990) Investment-banking contracts in tender o!ers: an empirical analysis. Journal of Financial Economics 28, 209-232.

Mikhail, M., Walther, B., Willis, R. (1998) Does forecast accuracy matter to analysts? Unpublished working paper, Massachusetts Institute of Technology, Cambridge, MA.

Perrone, T. & Laird, J. (2002) Fairness Opinions: What Are They? WhenAre They Needed?, Construction Law & Business Journal, 39-41.

Rau, P. R. (2000) Investment bank market share, contingent fee payments, and the performance of acquiring firms. Journal of Financial Economics, 56, 293-324.

Ruback, R. S. & Jensen, M. C. (1983) The Market for Corporate Control: The Scientific Evidence. Journal of Financial Economics, Vol. 11, pp. 5-50.

Schwetzler, B. & Aders, C. (2008) Jahrbuch der Unternehmensbewertung 2014: Know-how für Bewertungsprofessionals, Handelsblatt Fachmedien, Würzburg.

Servaes, H. & Zenner, M. (1996) The Role of Investment Banks in Acquisitions. Review of Financial Studies, 9, 787-815.

Shaked, I. & Kempainen, S. (2009) A Review of Fairness Opinions and Proxy Statements: 2005-2009. Journal of Applied Finance, 104-128.

Titman, S, and Trueman, B. (1986) Information Quality and the Valuation of New Issues,Journal of Accourting and Economics, 159-172.

4

SOCIAL COMPARISON AS A MEDIATOR VARIABLE BETWEEN COMMUNICATION DESIGN AND PURCHASE INTENTION

Agnieszka Michniuk

TABLE OF CONTENT

4.1 Introduction 93
4.2 Theoretical Background 95
4.3 Study Design 100
    4.3.1 Method 102
    4.3.2 Participants 103
    4.3.3 Results 105
4.4 Conclusion 114
References 115

4.1 Introduction

A marketing campaign which is criticized extremely in public nowadays is the campaign of Protein World[1]. Protein World wants to sell weight loss products by an advertisement which is showing a skinny woman in a bikini with the slogan "Are you beach body ready?". Since the start of the campaign two weeks ago thousands of people have signed to get these advertisements removed and forbidden as it is showing unrealistic body standards. These unrealistic standards could result in eating disorders or encourage woman to starve themselves.

Picture 1: Advertisement of Protein World in London Underground[2]

People are planning protests in London and even other companies are reacting to these ads like the company Dove. Dove is showing normal women in their advertisement in contrast to the idealized body picture of Protein World.

---

[1] Davies 2015.
[2] Bose 2015.

Picture 2: Advertisement of Dove in UK[1]

This popular outrage shows how important it is for marketers of a product to decide on which women to portray in an advertisement. Different portrayed women on ads may have different kind of effects on the consumers. This is what should be analyzed in the following study. The effect different kind of portrayed women have on female consumers.

---

[1] Theobald 2015.

4.2 Theoretical Background

In order to decide what effect portrayed woman in an ad have on female consumers and what the best marketing strategy might be the following model should be used (see graphic 1). Based on a reference point, which is the own position or in other words the position of the consumer who is looking at an ad, the product design may have an influence on three different kinds of things: the trust the consumer has in the product itself. Does the consumer believe that the producer will keep his promises? Will the consumer believe in its effectiveness? The second is social comparison. Will the consumer compare herself with the portrayed women? What kind of effect will this comparison process have on the consumer's motivation to buy the product? Last but not least and the most important one for marketers: the purchase intention. What kind of effect will the product design have on the purchase intention? Will the consumer be willing to buy the product? The buying intention might also be influenced by the result of the social comparison and by the fact if the consumer trusts the product or not.

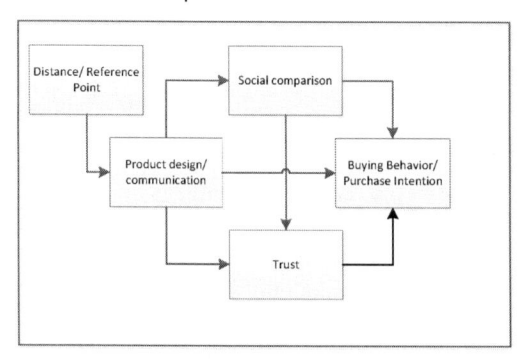

Graphic 1: Relationship between the product design and the purchase intention, mediated by social comparison and trust

In the following each individual construct will be explained shortly and hypothesis will be derived about the relationship of the constructs to each other, which will be tested in the subsequent study.

Marketers have to decide a couple of things when promoting a product: Which channel to choose to sell it, how to advertise it, by print media or TV spots, and for which target group it should be. Each decision, like for a specific brand communication, is resulting in consequences like a study in the area of mobile phones done by Azize et al. pointed out. Azize et al. figured out that there is an effect of brand communication on trust through brand satisfaction[2]. Therefore the following hypothesis can be derived:

H1: The product design/ communication has a positive effect on the trust of the buyer in the product and producer.

Like the protests against the advertisement of Protein World have shown the portrayed woman in an advertisement is important for the consumer as well. It can be assumed that when the consumer is feeling similar to the shown model and not that an unrealistic ideal is shown, they wouldn't protest against the campaign. This lead to the second hypothesis:

H2: The reference point is having an effect on the judgment of the advertisement. The closer the individual is to the shown model, the better is the rating of the product communication.

People have the tendency to compare themselves with others for different kind of reasons: They want to know how good they are in specific tasks, how they can become better in the future or just to keep a positive view of themselves. These three reasons can be described as motives for social comparison[3]. The first one, self-evaluation, is a judgment of one owns abilities, characteristics or appearance. The consumer is comparing himself to a beautiful model in an ad and deciding how well she or he looks compared to the model. The second motive, self-improvement, describes a comparison with a superior standard where the individual sets goals how he can reach this specific state. Imagine a TV spot for a tennis club with an old men playing tennis. The younger consumer might think he also wants to be still that active when he becomes older

---

[2] Azize et al. 2012, p. 1365.
[3] Martin/ Gentry 1997, p. 21.

and decides to join the tennis club as well. Last but not least, the self-enhancement motive of social comparison. In order to feel positive about oneself the consumer might avoid the comparison and decide that the end state that is shown to him is not realistic at all. Furthermore, previous studies like the study from Klesse et al. have shown that social comparison takes place when participants of a dieting program look at thin models on covers of dieting diaries[4]. In the current research the following hypothesis should be tested:

H3: The more attractive the model in the ad, the more social comparison will take place.

The Selective Accessibility Model of comparative thinking of Mussweiler stated that there are two different procedures individuals go through during the social comparison process: similarity or dissimilarity testing[5]. Similarity testing describes the focus on the characteristics of the comparison standard that are similar to one self. As opposed to similarity testing, dissimilarity testing means a focus on the differences between the comparison standard and one self[6]. Lockwood and Kunda assumed that it depends on the target itself, how attainable it is, if an assimilation or dissimilation occurs. That means if we look at a model in an ad and the weight or body of this model is attainable an assimilation effect occurs. This assimilation effect can be motivational and inspirational[7]. Therefore it can be stated:

H4: The greater the social comparison, the higher is the purchase intention.

Furthermore, based on the specific reference point a consumer is evaluating a product to be either positive and useful or negative and not worth buying[8]. Imagine the ad of Dove in UK with the normal weighted women. If somebody is also normal weighted the judgment will be positive of the advertisement as well as the consumers is seeing herself in the ad. This also may explain the negative feedback for the campaign of Protein World: Consumers are more likely to be normal weighted than extremely thin which result in a negative view

---

[4] Klesse et al. 2012, p. 355ff.
[5] Mussweiler 2003, p. 472f.
[6] Häfner 2004, p. 188f.
[7] Lockwood/ Kunda 1997, p. 93.
[8] Gierl / Stumpp 2000, p. 273.

and judgment of this ad that is seen as an unrealistic standard. From this observation the following hypothesis can be derived:

H5: The social comparison process will result in a higher rating of trust into the product.

The concept of trust have been in the focus of marketing and in many research papers over the past twenty years as customer-supplier relationships are always characterized by some kind of risk which can be eliminated by building up consumer trust.[9] As each buying situation is somehow risky, trust has also economic consequences for a company: The sales of a product will increase if the customers believe that the product will fulfill its obligations and promises.[10] Therefore it can be stated:

H6: The greater the trust in the product or the manufacturer, the greater the purchase intension.

However, it is not just the trust in the effectiveness that is important for marketers. Marketers want to motivate the consumers with their ads to buy a specific product. Therefore the product design should raise the wish to use the product. In other words the consumers should have the feeling that she could either solve a problem she has by using the product or reach a specific goal she has. In this context it doesn't matter what kind of goal it is, in the area of consumption products just the goal of being not hungry anymore. In the area of cosmetic products the goal could be to feel more attractive. Therefore the following hypothesis can be derived:

H7: The product design will have a positive influence on the consumer's purchase intention.

The following graphic gives a summary of all hypotheses or in other words an overview of the relationships between the latent variables.

---

[9] Akrout et al. 2011, p. 2; Akrout et al. 2011, p. 13.
[10] Akrout et al. 2011, p. 8.

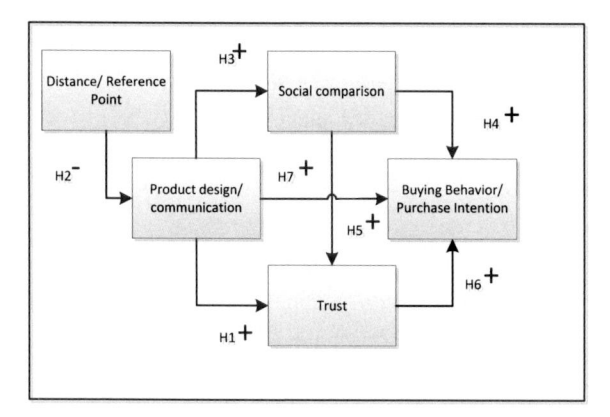

Graphic 2: Overview of the relationships between the latent variables of the model

4.3 STUDY DESIGN

In order to test the hypothesis above a questionnaire was designed. At the beginning of each questionnaire one of four different kinds of ads has been shown. Each ad displayed a woman next to the product. There have been two ads for a skin care products and two for ads for fashion. The two categories skin care and fashion haven't been chosen for a specific reason and could have been replaced by any other product category. The important criterion in the selection process for a proper ad was to have women displayed with a different type of figure and weight. The participants have been divided randomly into four different experimental groups, this happened when they clicked on the online link to participate in the questionnaire by the survey tool. The following table gives an overview of the characteristics of each individual experimental group:

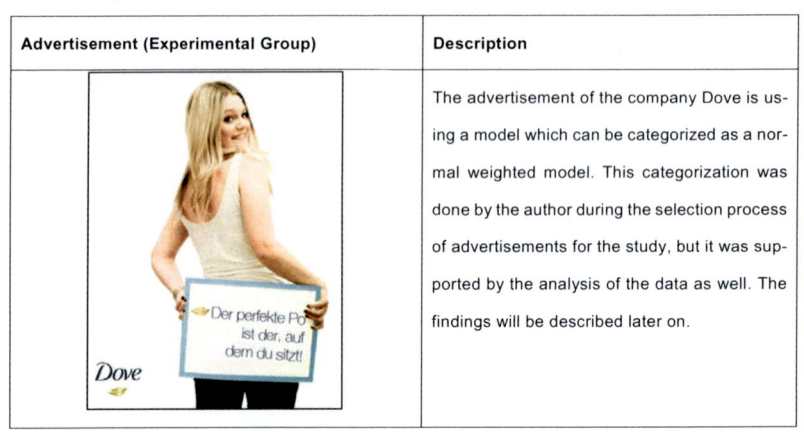

Advertisement (Experimental Group)	Description
	The advertisement of the company Dove is using a model which can be categorized as a normal weighted model. This categorization was done by the author during the selection process of advertisements for the study, but it was supported by the analysis of the data as well. The findings will be described later on.

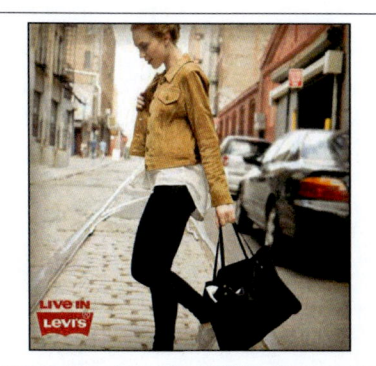

(Levis ad image)	The advertisement of the company Levis is using a model which can be categorized as a thin model. It seems easy to see that the Levis model is thinner than the model used for the Dove ad. This categorization, which was done during the selection process of an advertisement with a thin model by the author, was confirmed by the analysis of the results as well.
 (Nivea ad image)	The advertisement of the company Nivea is using a model which was categorized as normal weighted model. However, the normal weighted Nivea model is thinner than the model used for the Dove advertisement. This pre-defined categorization can be confirmed by the questionnaire results as well.
(Zizzi ad image)	The advertisement of the company Zizzi is using a model which was categorized as a moderate thick model. The model is heavier than all the other models used in the three other ads. This assumption or categorization was supported by the test results as well.

The questions in the questionnaire have been the same regardless of the advertisement which the participant saw at the beginning. The main parts of the questionnaire have been the following: Determination of the reference point, the judgment of the advertisement (product design/ communication), evaluation of own social comparison behavior, trust ratings as well as the judgment of one owns buying intention. Last but not least some personal questions about the age, weight, size, social status and gender have been asked.

4.3.1 METHOD

The questionnaire was answered online by the participants that will allow a fast and easy evaluation of the results. Next to that the time period of the participation should be one week. This time frame should allow getting a sufficient number of participants. The online link to the questionnaire was sent to female friends, colleagues and other students of the FOM Hochschule für Oekonomie & Management. As the participation was voluntary and there was no monetary incentive, the hope was to get sufficient participants by asking in the circle of acquaintances. The participation was anonymous and the data was treated confidential. In order to minimize the problem of response bias some of the questions have been asked in an inverse way. This can be used to check if the participants have been attentive all the time. In order to measure each construct multiple items have been used. All items have been taken from previous studies and have been judged as reliable. As there are different views on the number of items needed per construct (e.g. Churchill is mentioning 10 items[1], Peter is stating that half of the studies are taking 3-6 items[2], Bollen said that 3-4 items are enough[3]) the number of items per construct varies between 5-15. Concerning Weiber/ Mühlhaus it is advisable to use four to nine point scales[4]. Furthermore, Miller stated that participants can only distinguish in a reliable way scales of 7 plus/minus 2 graduations[5]. Therefore it was decided that for nearly all of the questions a seven point Likert scale was used with the end points 1= I strongly disagree and 7= I strongly agree. Only for measuring the distance of the participant to the model itself another type of scale was used (see graphic 3). Hereby the participants should compare the body mass index (BMI) of the model shown in the ad with the own BMI. The end points of the scale have been -10= lower BMI and +10= higher BMI. In the results -10 was coded as 1 and +10 as 101, therefore 51 was the mean (shown as zero in the scale). In order to have the distance independent of the direction

---

[1] Churchill 1979, p. 69.
[2] Peter 1979, p. 12f.
[3] Bollen 1989, p. 288ff.
[4] Weiber/ Mühlhaus 2014, p. 116.
[5] Miller 1956, p. 81ff.

the following calculation was done: (51 − coded value) * (-1). As a result, 0 denoting no distance and 50 maximum distance.

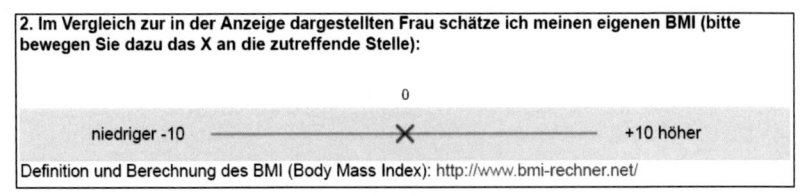

2. Im Vergleich zur in der Anzeige dargestellten Frau schätze ich meinen eigenen BMI (bitte bewegen Sie dazu das X an die zutreffende Stelle):
niedriger -10 ——————————X—————————— +10 höher   (0)
Definition und Berechnung des BMI (Body Mass Index): http://www.bmi-rechner.net/

Graphic 3: Scale to measure the distance/ reference point

In total 296 questionnaires have been completed by the participants. However, not all of them have been completed fully as just the first few questions have been mandatory. As some of the not-mandatory questions have been important for the analysis, just 234 questionnaires have been used as they contain answers to most of the questions. This number fulfils the sample size requirement defined by Chin, who recommended using five to ten times the number of indicators of the construct with the highest number of items[6]. As the construct "producer trust" has the highest number of items (7 indicators) the sample size should be at least between 35 and 70.

4.3.2 PARTICIPANTS

As the shown ads displayed only woman the target group of the questionnaire have also been woman. This was important as some of the questions like about the social comparison behavior can only be answered by woman. In order to be sure that just women took part in the questionnaire, the participants had to select their gender in the personal questions part.

---

[6] Chin 1998, p. 311.

The following table gives an overview of the participants in each group. There is no significant difference between the experimental groups in the BMI (F = 0,687, n.s.) or age (F – 0,403, n.s.). Next to that, the number per group is similar. As the BMI is nearly the same per group the rating of the distance to the shown model, which was part of the questionnaire, represents the categorization of the model itself (see Table 1).

Group	Number of participants	Average BMI	Distance	Average age
Dove	61	22,421	-3,377	27,97
Levis	61	22,016	15,115	28,21
Nivea	56	22,210	9,125	28,11
Zizzi	56	22,929	-19,589	29,39

Table1: Overview of the characteristics of each experimental group. The value of the distance can be negative or positive in relation to the neutral position 51.

The following graphic, which shows the average BMI per experimental group in comparison to the rated distance of the individual to the model, supports the predefined categorization of the models. The distance in this context means the distance from the zero point of the scale. Zero represent that the individual's BMI is the same like the BMI of the model. Negative values mean that the BMI is lower, positive ones that the BMI is higher of the individual compared to the model.

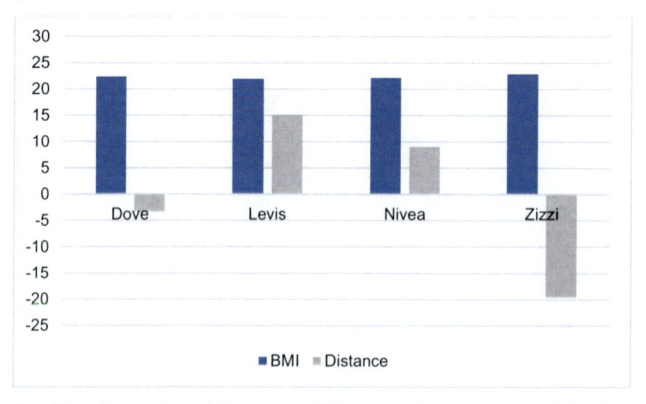

Graphic 4: Comparison of the average BMI per experimental group and the distance ratings.

Compared to the Dove model the participants rated their BMI as a little bit lower. This supports the pre-categorization that the Dove model is normal weighted but a little bit heavier than the Nivea model. Compared to the Nivea model the participants rated their BMI as higher. So this confirms the assumption as well. The most explicit results show the distance rating to the Zizzi and Levis model. The BMI was rated as much lower for the Zizzi model which is represented by a distance value of -19,589, and much higher for the Levis model (distance value of 15,115).

4.3.3 RESULTS

Based on the type of model, if it is formative or reflective, there are a couple of different statistical testing procedures. In a formative model all items or indicators are the result of the construct. In contrast, in a reflective model all indicators or items are the cause of the construct[7]. As it will be assumed that the underlying model is a reflective one, the following statistical testing procedures will be applied in the following in order to evaluate the measurement and structural modell:

- Cronbach's Alpha
- Indicator reliability
- Convergence criteria
    - Average Variance Extracted (AVE)
    - Composite Reliability
- Discriminant validity
    - Fornell- Larcker Criterion
    - Cross Loadings
- Path coefficients
- R Square (R^2)
- Collinearity Statistic (Inner Variance Inflation Factor (VIF))
Stone- Geisser- Criterion (Q^2)

---

[7] Eberl 2004, p. 2ff.

4.3.3.1 EVALUATION OF THE MEASUREMENT MODELL

The operationalization of the construct "communication design" was done by six items which are shown in table 2. Values for Cronbach's Alpha are within the interval [0;1]. The closer the value gets to 1 the more reliable is the indicator[8]. For the construct "communication design" Cronbach's Alpha is very high with a value of 0,933. This value is above the threshold value of 0,7, which is used in the literature for constructs with four or more items[9]. Furthermore, Nunnally advices to use an indicator set only if Cronbach's Alpha is above 0,7[10]. To sum up, the measuring model for the construct "communication design" can be described as reliable because of this high Cronbach's Alpha value. Next to that, table 1 shows the indicator reliability values for each variable. The indicator reliability is the explained variance of an indicator. The value of the indicator reliability, which ranges from 0 to 1, should be above 0,4 (or even better above 0,6)[11]. All indicators of the construct communication design have an indicator reliability value above 0,6 except one variable, which was removed from the model.

There are two convergence criteria: The Average Variance Extracted (AVE) and the Composite Reliability. The AVE values are within the interval [0;1]. The closer the value gets to 1 the more reliable is the indicator. The threshold value for AVE is above 0,5[12]. The AVE for the construct is 0,749 and is therefore above the threshold value. For the Composite Reliability the threshold value is above 0,7[13]. The Composite Reliability for the construct is 0,947.

---

[8] Nieschlag 2002, p. 428.
[9] Ohlwein 1999, p. 224.
[10] Nunnally 1994, p. 252.
[11] Peter 1999, p.145.
[12] Bagozzi/ Yi 1988, p. 82.
[13] Bagozzi/ Yi 1988, p. 82.

Variable	Indicators for communication design	Indicator reliability	T-Value
CD01_01	Die Werbeanzeige dieses Produkts gefällt mir sehr gut.	0,893	47,845
CD01_02	Die Werbeanzeige dieses Produkts stimmt mich sehr positiv.	0,877	48,996
CD01_03	Die Werbeanzeige dieses Produkts finde ich sehr ansprechend.	0,917	73,158
CD01_04	Die Werbeanzeige dieses Produkts stimmt mich glücklich.	0,826	36,468
CD01_06	Diese Werbeanzeige ist gut gemacht.	0,860	46,335
CD01_07	Diese Werbeanzeige ist interessant.	0,815	31,571
Cronbach's Alpha: 0,933; Average Variance Extracted (AVE): 0,749; Composite Reliability: 0,947.			

Table 2: Construct "Communication design" - reflective

Table 2 and Table 3 shows the operationalization of the construct "trust" which was split into two constructs producer and product trust. The value for Cronbach's Alpha for the construct "product trust" is quite high with a value of 0,858, which is also above the threshold value of 0,7. Consequently, the measuring model for the construct "product trust" is reliable as well. Furthermore, all indicators of the construct "trust" have an indicator reliability value above 0,6. Indicators who had values below 0,7 have been removed from this construct as well. The AVE for the construct is 0,638 and is therefore above the threshold value of 0,5. Furthermore, the T-Value of all indicators is above the threshold value of 1,96

Variable	Indicators for product trust	Indicator reliability	T-Value
TR01_01	Das beworbene Produkt hält vermutlich was es verspricht.	0,842	27,951
TR01_02	Das beworbene Produkt wirkt vertrauenswürdig.	0,837	36,455
TR01_03	Das beworbene Produkt erfüllt vermutlich seinen Zweck.	0,784	17,586
TR01_04	Das beworbene Produkt wird vermutlich allen Nutzerinnen gefallen.	0,754	22,293
TR01_07	Das beworbene Produkt erfüllt wohl genau meine Erwartungen.	0,772	20,487
Cronbachs Alpha: 0,858; Average Variance Extracted (AVE): 0,638; Composite Reliability: 0,898.			

Table 3: Construct "Product trust" - reflective

The following table shows the results for the construct "producer trust". The value for Cronbach's Alpha for this construct is quite high with a value of 0,899, which is also above the threshold value of 0,7. Furthermore, all indicators of the construct have an indicator reliability value above 0,6. Indicators who had values below 0,7 have been removed from this construct as well. The AVE for the construct is 0,634 and is therefore above the threshold value of 0,5. Furthermore, the T-Value of all indicators is above the threshold value of 1,96. Consequently, this construct can be described as reliable.

Variable	Indicators for producer trust	Indicator reliability	T-Value
TR02_01	Der Hersteller bietet mir ein Produkt mit konstanter Qualität an.	0,739	19,981
TR02_02	Der Hersteller würde mir vermutlich weiterhelfen, wenn es Probleme mit seinem Produkt gibt (z. B. bei Reklamationen).	0,804	28,734
TR02_03	Der Hersteller bietet mir ein brauchbares neues Produkt an.	0,782	19,557
TR02_04	Der Hersteller sorgt für meine Zufriedenheit.	0,857	35,284
TR02_05	Der Hersteller schätzt mich als Käuferin seines Produkts.	0,782	21,867
TR02_06	Der Hersteller kümmert sich um seine Kundinnen.	0,783	21,565
TR02_07	Ich vertraue der Information, die der Hersteller zur Verfügung stellt.	0,776	23,990
Cronbachs Alpha: 0,899; Average Variance Extracted (AVE): 0,624; Composite Reliability: 0,921.			

Table 4: Construct "Producer trust" - reflective

The operationalization of the construct "social comparison" is done by three items which are shown in the following table. The value for Cronbach's Alpha for this construct is quite low with a value of 0,887, which is above the threshold value of 0,7. Consequently, the measuring model for the construct "social comparison" is reliable like the two constructs before. Five indicators of the construct "social comparison" had an indicator reliability value below 0,6 and have been therefore removed in the model. The AVE for the construct is 0,816 and is below the threshold value of 0,5. Furthermore, the T-Value of all indicators is above the threshold value of 1,96.

Variable	Indicators for social comparison	Indicator reliability	T-Value
SC01_01	Wenn ich Frauen in der Werbung sehe, denke ich fast immer darüber nach, wie gut oder schlecht ich im Vergleich zu ihnen aussehe.	0,894	45,215
SC01_02	Ich wünsche mir oft, dass ich aussehe wie Frauen in der Werbung.	0,918	60,213
SC01_03	Ich vergleiche mich sehr häufig mit Frauen, die eine bessere Figur haben.	0,897	43,194
Cronbach's Alpha: 0,887; Average Variance Extracted (AVE): 0,816; Composite Reliability: 0,930.			

Table 5: Construct "Social comparison" - reflective

The operationalization of the construct "purchase intention" is done by five items which are shown in table 4. The value for Cronbach's Alpha for this construct is very high with a value of 0,913, which is above the threshold value of 0,7. Therefore, the measuring of this construct can be evaluated as reliable. The indicator reliability of all indicators for the construct "purchase intention" is above the threshold value of 0,6. This also supports the statement that the indicators are reliable. The AVE for the construct is 0,747 and is therefore above the threshold value, which is an evidence for reliability.

Variable	Indicators for purcase intension	Indicator reliability	T-Value
PI01_01	Die Wahrscheinlichkeit, dass dieses Produkt bei einem Kauf für mich in Frage kommt, ist sehr hoch.	0,867	54,708
PI01_02	Wenn ich Produkte dieser Warengruppe kaufen würde, entscheide ich mich für das in der Werbeanzeige dargestellte Produkt.	0,728	16,510
PI01_03	Die Wahrscheinlichkeit, dass ich dieses Produkt kaufe, ist hoch.	0,944	103,417
PI01_04	Meine Bereitschaft, dieses Produkt zu kaufen, ist hoch.	0,931	26,106
PI01_05	Ich werde dieses Produkt in Zukunft verwenden.	0,837	45,215
Cronbach's Alpha: 0,913; Average Variance Extracted (AVE): 0,747; Composite Reliability: 0,936.			

Table 6: Construct "Purchase intention" - reflective

The next statistical testing criteria, which is analyzed is the discriminant validity. Herefore the Fornell- Larcker Criterion and the Cross Loadings will be used. Based on Fornell/ Larcker the discriminant validity is existent if the Average Extracted Variance (AVE) is higher than the squared correlation between two latent variables, which can be interpreted as the shared variance of the two constructs[14]. Table 7 gives an overview of the correlations. It can be stated that the AVE is higher than the squared correlation between the constructs, therefore the discriminant validity is given.

	Comm. Design	Producer trust	Product trust	Purchase Intention
Producer trust	0,145			
Product trust	0,256	0,366		
Purchase Intention	0,203	0,250	0,299	
Social Comparison	0,036	0,067	0,049	0,098

Table 7: Squared correlation between latent variables

---

[14] Fornell/ Larcker 1981, p. 46.

The following table shows the cross loadings for each indicator of all constructs. As each indicator has a higher loading on the corresponding construct for which it was used than on other constructs, the discriminant validity is given[15].

Variable	Comm. Design	Producer trust	Product trust	Purchase Intention	Social Comparison
"CD01_01"	0,893	0,313	0,440	0,323	0,182
"CD01_02"	0,877	0,330	0,410	0,408	0,124
"CD01_03"	0,917	0,362	0,457	0,404	0,138
"CD01_04"	0,826	0,374	0,438	0,438	0,160
"CD01_06"	0,860	0,250	0,451	0,330	0,185
"CD01_07"	0,815	0,332	0,428	0,415	0,207
"PI01_01"	0,460	0,522	0,596	0,867	0,336
"PI01_02"	0,320	0,438	0,392	0,728	0,253
"PI01_03"	0,417	0,394	0,449	0,944	0,305
"PI01_04"	0,403	0,411	0,444	0,931	0,250
"PI01_05"	0,307	0,364	0,444	0,837	0,172
"SC01_01"	0,178	0,235	0,203	0,270	0,894
"SC01_02"	0,174	0,245	0,188	0,295	0,918
"SC01_03"	0,167	0,222	0,209	0,282	0,897
"TR01_01"	0,406	0,476	0,842	0,399	0,100
"TR01_02"	0,502	0,533	0,837	0,449	0,235
"TR01_03"	0,315	0,428	0,784	0,375	0,062
"TR01_04"	0,400	0,464	0,754	0,429	0,261
"TR01_07"	0,367	0,498	0,772	0,520	0,195
"TR02_01"	0,306	0,739	0,469	0,343	0,280
"TR02_02"	0,261	0,804	0,400	0,357	0,207
"TR02_03"	0,269	0,782	0,509	0,374	0,171
"TR02_04"	0,351	0,857	0,574	0,453	0,204
"TR02_05"	0,317	0,782	0,423	0,429	0,192
"TR02_06"	0,334	0,783	0,410	0,426	0,211
"TR02_07"	0,259	0,776	0,532	0,375	0,173

Table 8: Cross loadings

---

[15] Chin 1998, p. 321 f.

4.3.3.2 EVALUATION OF THE STRUCTURAL MODELL

Path coefficients are in the range of -1 to 1, where values higher than 0,1 or below -0,1 have an influence that can't be undervalued concerning Lohmöller[16]. Chin claims that values above 0,2 until 0,3 represent a significant influence[17]. Graphic 4 shows the final structural equation model with values for the path coefficients for all constructs. The highest influence has the product trust on the producer trust (0,533), the communication design on the product trust (0,481) and the producer trust on the purchase intention (0,348). There only one negative path coefficient between distance and communication design (-0,130). This seems to make sense because a higher value for the distance represents a higher distance to the model shown in the ad, which results in a negative evaluation of the advertisement. All path coefficients are showing a significant influence of latent variable on the following variable.

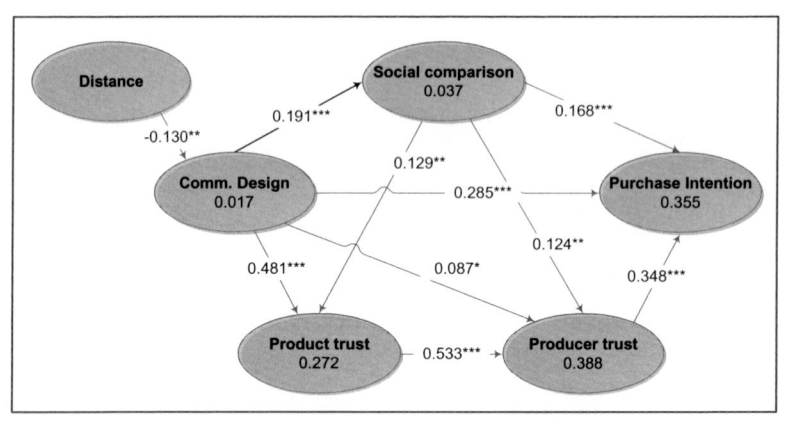

Graphic 5: Path coefficients (***p<.01; **p<.05; *p<.1 (one-tailed); n=234)

---

[16] Lohmoller 1989, p. 60f.
[17] Chin 1998a, p.11.

R Square is the percentage of the explained variance in relationship to the total variance. Graphic 5 shows also the values for R Square for all constructs. R Square values are within the range of [0;1]. Values above 0,67 are categorized as a substantial, between 0,67 and 0,33 as good in average and between 0,33 and 0,19 as weak. Therefore the producer trust (0,388) and the purchase intention (0,355) are good in average. The value for the product trust can be described as weak (0,272). The R Square values for social comparison and communication design are even below the lower limit of the weak range of 0,19.

Table 9 shows the inner VIF values (VIF = Variance Inflation Factor) for all exogen constructs, which should be close to 1 and far away from 10^{18}. This seems to be the case for all VIF values. Therefore no multi- collinearity is present, which means the constructs are independent from each other.

	Comm. Design	DistanzRF	Producer trust	Product trust	Purchase Intention	Social Comparison
Comm. Design			1,038	1,356	1,182	1,000
DistanzRF	1,000					
Producer trust				1,374		
Product trust					1,221	
Social Comparison			1,038	1,061	1,084	

Table 9: Inner VIF Values

Finally, the Stone- Geisser – Criterion (Q^2), which can be used for reflective latent constructs which are endogenous, can give insight into the forecasting relevance.[19] If the value for Q^2 is above 1 the model contains forecasting relevance, if it is below 1 it doesn't. A value of zero means that the model isn't better than an estimation of the data done by the mean[20].

The only endogenous variable in the model is the purchase intention. All other variables are exogenous. The Q^2 value for the purchase intention after doing the blindfolding is 0,238. Therefore the forecasting relevance can be confirmed.

---

[18] Gansser/ Kroll 2015, p. 159.
[19] Weiber/ Mühlhaus 2014, p. 329.
[20] Weiber/ Mühlhaus 2014, p. 329.

4.4 General Discussion

The result shows that nearly all seven hypotheses can be accepted. The first hypothesis stated that the product design/ communication has a positive effect on the trust of the buyer in the product and producer. The effect on the product trust is significant (0,481) whereas the effect on the producer trust isn't (0,087). Therefore only the first part can be accepted and the second rejected.

The second hypothesis claimed that the reference point is having an effect on the judgment of the advertisement. The closer the individual is to the shown model, the better is the rating of the product communication. This hypothesis can be accepted as well. The path coefficient is negative (-0,130) because higher distance values represent a higher distance between the individual and the model and result in a worse rating of the product design.

The product design or the image shown in ad lead to social comparison, which was claimed by hypothesis 3, can be confirmed as well.

The fourth hypothesis stated that the social comparison process will result in a higher buying intention, what was confirmed by a positive path coefficient of 0,168. Furthermore, the social comparison process also results in a higher rating of trust into the product as well as into the producer.

The positive relationship between trust and the consumer's willingness to buy a specific product, which was claimed by hypothesis 6, can be confirmed as well.

Next to the effects of the product design on the trust and social comparison, there is also a direct effect which the product design has on willingness to buy the product (path coefficient of 0,285).

References

Akrout, W.; Akrout, H. (2011): Trust in B-to-B: Toward a Dynamic and Integrative Approach. In: Recherche et Applications en Marketing, Vol. 26, No. 1 (2011), pp. 1-21.

Azize, S. / Cemal, Z. / Hakan, K. (2012): Does Brand Communication increases Brand Trust? The Empirical Research on Global Mobile Phone Brands. Social and Behavioral Sciences 58 (2012), p. 1361 – 1369.

Bagozzi, R. P. / Yi, Y. (1988): On the Evaluation of Structural Equation Models. Journal of the Academy of Marketing Science, 16(1), 74–94.

Bollen, K. A. (1989): Structural equations with latent variables. New York: Wiley-Interscience.

Bose, A. (2015): 'Are You Beach Body Ready?': Ad Pulled After Being Slammed as Body-Shaming. NDTV, http://www.ndtv.com/offbeat/are-you-beach-body-ready-ad-pulled-after-being-slammed-as-body-shaming-759176, 28.04.2015

Chae, B./ Li, X./ Zhu, R. (2013): Judging Product Effectiveness from Perceived Spatial Proximity. Journal of Consumer Research, Vol. 40, No. 2, p. 317-335.

Chin, W. W. (1998a). Issues and opinion on structural equation modeling. Management Information Systems Quarterly, 22, 7–16.

Chin, W. W. (1998b): The Partial Least Squares Approach to Structural Equation Modeling, in: Marcoulides, G. (Hrsg.): Modern Business Research Methods, New Jersey, S. 295-336.

Churchill, G. A. (1979): A paradigm for developing better measures for marketing constructs. Journal of Marketing Research, 16, p. 64-73.

Davies, C. (2015): 'Beach body ready' tube advert protests planned for Hyde Park. The Guardian, http://www.theguardian.com/media/2015/apr/27/mass-demonstration-planned-over-beach-body-ready-tube-advert, 28.04.2015

Eberl, M. (2004): Formative und reflektive Indikatoren im Forschungsprozess: Entscheidungsregeln und die Dominanz des reflektiven Modells. Schriften zur Empirischen Forschung und Quantitativen Unternehmensplanung, Bd. 19. München.

Fornell, C., / Larcker, D. F. (1981). Evaluation structural equation models with unobservable variables and measurement error. Journal of Marketing Research, 18, 39–50.

Gansser, O. / Kroll, B. (2015): Ein Modell zur Erklärung und Prognose des Werbeplanungserfolgs. Springer Fachmedien Wiesbaden.

Gierl, H. / Stumpp, S. (2000): Erklärung und Beeinflussung von Referenzniveaus. in: Marketing ZFP, 22. Jg., Heft 4/2000, S. 273-295.

Häfner, M. (2004): How dissimilar others may still resemble the self: Assimilation and contrast after social comparison. Journal of Consumer Psychology, Vol. 14, No.1/ 2, p. 187- 196.

Klesse, A.-K./ Goukens, C./ Geyskens, K./ Ruyter, K. de (2012): Repeated exposure to the thin ideal and implications for the self: Two weight loss program studies. International Journal of Research in Marketing, Vol. 29, No.4, p. 355- 362.

Lockwood, P. / Kunda, Z. (1997). Superstars and me: Predicting the impact of role models on the self. Journal of Personality and Social Psychology, 73, 91-103.

Lohmoller, J. B. (1989). Latent variable path modeling with partial least squares. Heidelberg: Physica.

Martin, M. C. / Gentry, J.W. (1997): Stuck in the Model Trap: The Effects of Beautiful Models in Ads on Female Pre-Adolescents and Adolescents. Journal of Advertising, Vol. 26, No. 2, pp. 19-34.

Miller, G. A. (1956): The magical number seven, plus or minus two: Some limits on our capacity for processing information. Psychological Review, 63, p. 81- 97.

Mussweiler, T. (2003): Comparison processes in social judgment: Mechanisms and consequences. Psychological Review, 110, 472-489.

Nieschlag, R./ Dichtl, E./ & Hörschgen, H. (2002). Marketing (19. Aufl.). Berlin.

Nunnally, J. C./ Bernstein, I. H. (1994). Psychometric theory (3. Aufl.). New York: McGraw-Hill.

Ohlwein, M. (1999): Märkte für gebrauchte Güter. Wiesbaden.

Peter, J. P. (1979): Reliability: A review of psychometric basics and recent marketing practices. Journal of Marketing Research, 26, p. 6-17.

Peter, S. I. (1999): Kundenbindung als Marketingziel (2. Aufl.).Wiesbaden.

Theobald, T. (2015): Dümmliche Beachbody-Anzeige sorgt für Proteste in Londoner U-Bahn. Horizont, http://www.horizont.net/marketing/nachrichten/Protein-World-Duemmliche-Beachbody-Anzeige-sorgt-fuer-Proteste-in-Londoner-U-Bahn-134122, 28.04.2015

Weiber, R./ Mühlhaus, D. (2014): Strukturgleichungsmodellierung. Springer Verlag. Berlin Heidelberg.

5

DIGITALIZATION AND MOTION PICTURES: A THEATRICAL MARKET ANALYSIS

Florian Wrobel

TABLE OF CONTENT

5.1 Introduction 119
    5.1.1 Problem Definition 119
    5.1.2 Research Objectives 120
    5.1.3 Methodology 120
    5.1.4 Thesis outline 122
5.2 Theatrical market analysis 123
    5.2.1 Theatrical market overview 123
    5.2.2 Revenues from foreign markets 127
    5.2.3 Creativity in Hollywood 130
5.3 Summary and Outlook 134
    5.3.1 Summary 134
    5.3.2 Outlook 135
References 138

5.1 INTRODUCTION

5.1.1. PROBLEM DEFINITION

The motion picture industry has witnessed tremendous technological advancements in the last two decades. Examples include the switch from analog to digital production processes, the conversion of cinemas worldwide to digital projection as well as the increasing consumption of movies over the internet – legally and illegally.

These dramatic changes prompted several industry practitioners to share their view on the state of the motion picture industry in recent years – and for many of them, Hollywood is completely broken.[1] The drastic transformation started in 2008 with the decline of the DVD business. This led to a situation where studios are now heavily dependent on foreign markets for profits. This dependence, in turn, directly influences the type of motion pictures that are being made - as it is easier to market motion pictures, which are based on established properties and well known stars.[2]

---

[1] Popular examples include Lynda Obst's book *Sleepless in Hollywood* released in 2013, cp. Obst, L. (2013); a widely reported speech by Steven Spielberg and George Lucas about the Implosion of Hollywood in the same year, cp. THR (2013), w/o p., last accessed 24.03.2015; and a Variety column labelled *Broken Hollywood* in which multiple industry insiders share their opinions on the state of Hollywood, cp. Variety (2015), w/o p., last accessed 24.03.2015.

[2] Cp. Obst, L. (2013), pp. 36-41.

5.1.2 Research Objectives

The objective of the thesis is to analyze the changes that have occurred on the theatrical market in the past fifteen years. This includes an analysis of how certain aspects of the product - the motion picture itself - have changed.

By using quantitative data, the following research questions will be answered in the course of the analysis:

- How important are revenues from foreign markets for Hollywood Studios and how has the importance changed in the past 15 years?
- Has Hollywood lost its' creativity? Are Studios increasingly producing sequels and/or franchise movies based on established properties?

5.1.3 Methodology

In order to be able quantify the changes of the past fifteen years, for each year from 1999 to 2014, data for the one hundred motion pictures with the highest domestic revenues (1500 movies in total)[3] has been collected. This is a particular interesting time frame for the motion picture industry as the year 1999 saw the rise of the DVD followed by the start of the transition to digital projection shortly after. The new millennium then introduced additional technological advancements, like the introduction of the Blu-Ray as well as an increase in options to download or stream motion pictures over the internet.

---

[3] In the years 1999-2014 a total of 8909 motion pictures were released domestically, cp. Figure 4

For each motion picture, the following meta-data has been collected:

- Domestic Ranking[4]
- Movie title
- Studio / Distributor
- Worldwide revenues in U.S. dollars
- Domestic revenues in U.S. dollars and as percentage of worldwide revenues
- Foreign revenues in U.S. dollars and as percentage of worldwide revenues
- Genre
- MPAA rating
- Source (based on)
- Part of franchise?
- Sequel?
- Production budget in U.S. dollars
- Runtime (in minutes)
- Number of domestic theaters (total)
- Number of domestic theaters (opening weekend)
- Domestic revenues (opening weekend) in U.S. dollars
- Number of countries the movie is released in

Due to the limited scope of this thesis, not all the meta-data collected will be incorporate into the analysis. This thesis is part of larger research project, which will use the findings and data produced by this thesis as additional input.[5]

---

[4] USA / Canada
[5] Chapter 5.3.2 provides an outlook on the main research project.

5.1.4 THESIS OUTLINE

This thesis consists of three main parts: (I) the introduction in Chapter 5.1; (II) the analysis of the theatrical market and the product in Chapter 5.2 and (III) the summary and outlook in Chapter 5.3.

The analysis of the theatrical market in Chapter 5.2 is divided into further sub chapters. In Chapter 5.2.1 a general overview of the theatrical market will be given. In Chapter 5.2.2 the focus will then shift towards the first research question – the importance of foreign revenues. Chapter 5.2.3 is devoted to the second research questions – the possible loss of creativity.

This thesis concludes in Chapter 5.3, where the findings of the analysis will be summed up and an outlook on the main research project will be given. The literary sources used in this thesis are referenced at the end of this chapter. This thesis has no appendices.

5.2 THEATRICAL MARKET ANALYSIS

5.2.1 THEATRICAL MARKET OVERVIEW

In order to introduce the reader to the motion picture industry and the theatrical market, the following paragraphs will provide a general market overview. The data in this sub chapter is based on reports provided annually by the Motion Picture Association of America (MPAA). The values include all movies released worldwide, regardless of distributor or country of origin.

Figure 1 gives an overview of the domestic and foreign box office revenues of the last 15 years. The numbers at the bottom (blue) represent the domestic[6] box office revenues whereas the top row (red) shows the foreign box office revenues.

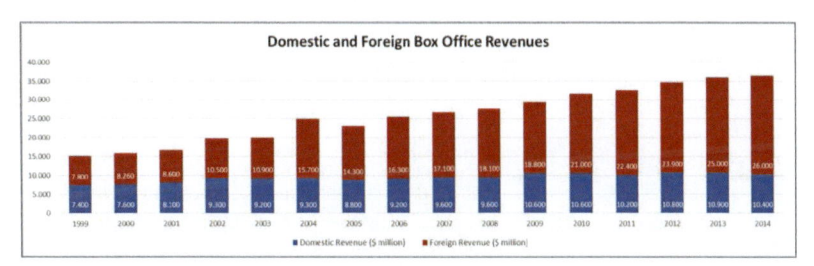

Fig.1: Domestic and Foreign Box Office Revenues, based on: MPA (2006), pp. 4-5; MPA (2003), p. 4; MPAA (2015), p. 4; MPAA (2010), p. 3.

The global box office[7] reached $36.4 billion in 2014[8] an increase of 139% when compared to the $15.2 billion reached in 1999[9] - an average annual growth rate of 9.2%.

---

[6] USA / Canada.
[7] The values for the Global Box Office include all movies released, regardless of distributor or country of origin, cp. MPAA (2015), p. 4, last accessed: 24.05.2015.
[8] Cp. MPAA (2015), p. 4, last accessed: 24.05.2015.
[9] Cp. MPA (2003), p. 4, last accessed: 24.05.2015.

The differentiation between domestic and foreign box office revenues gives a more nuanced picture: In 2014 the foreign box office ($26.0 billion) accounted for 72% of global box office revenues.[10] In 1999, the foreign box office revenues ($7.8 billion) were only slightly higher than the domestic box office revenues ($7.4 billion) and accounted for only 51% of global box office revenues.[11] This represents an increase in the share of the global box office by 21% in the last 15 years.

As can be seen in Figure 1, it is the foreign box office revenues that have been the growth driver for the global box office in the last fifteen years. Foreign box office revenues in U.S. dollars[12] are up 4% compared to 2013, 24% over five years ago[13] and 233% over fifteen years ago. Global box office revenues are up 15% and 139% respectively in the same time period.

While not shown, the foreign growth is driven primarily by the Asia Pacific region (up 12% from 2013). Chinese box office ($4.8 billion) increased 34% in 2014 and became the first international market to exceed $4 billion in box office revenues.[14]

The domestic box office, on the other hand, was actually down 5% from $10.9 billion in 2013 to $10.4 billion in 2014. Admissions, or tickets sold (1.27 billion) also declined 6% in 2014 when compared to 2013 (1.34 billion tickets sold)[15] and 13% compared to 1999. The development of domestic ticket sales is shown in Figure 2.

---

[10] Cp. MPAA (2015), p. 4, last accessed: 24.05.2015.
[11] Cp. MPA (2003), p. 4, last accessed: 24.05.2015.
[12] For a discussion on the impact of swings in foreign-currency exchange rates on the profitability of U.S. studios, cp. Vogel, H.L. (2011), pp. 87-92.
[13] Cp. MPAA (2015), p. 4, last accessed: 24.05.2015.
[14] Cp. MPAA (2015), p. 5, last accessed: 24.05.2015.
[15] Cp. MPAA (2015), p. 9, last accessed: 24.05.2015.

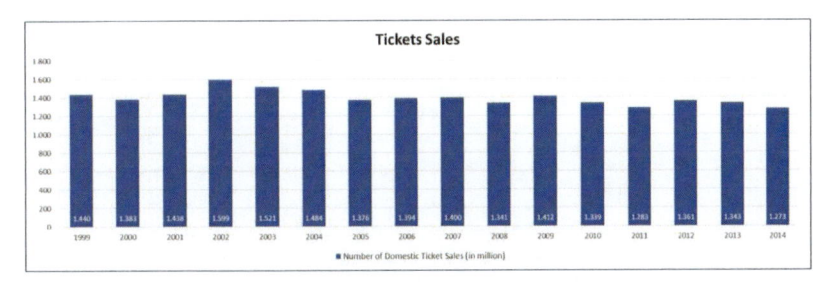

Fig.2: Domestic Ticket Sales, based on: MPA (2006), p. 6; MPAA (2015), p. 9.

In order to be able to put the decrease in ticket sales into perspective. Figure 3 shows the development of ticket prices in the last fifteen years. The average ticket price in 1999 was $5.08[16], in 2014 the average ticket price was $8.17, an increase of $3.09 or 61% in the last fifteen years. When compared to 2013, the average ticket price increased by 4 cents (less than 1%) in 2014, which is less than the 2% increase in inflation as measured by the Consumer Price Index (CPI).[17]

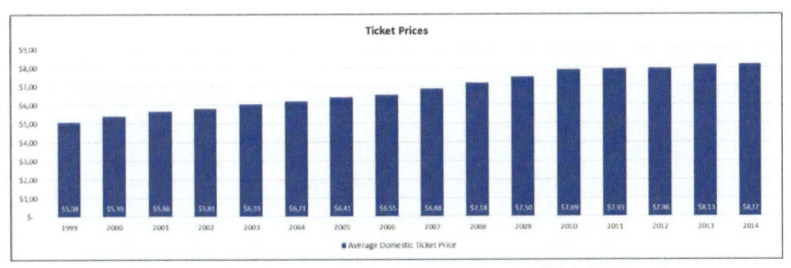

Fig.3: Average Domestic Ticket Prices, based on: MPA (2006), p. 6; MPAA (2015), p. 9.

To conclude the general market overview, it is also important to understand, how many movies are released per year and who is releasing them. Figure 4 shows how many motion pictures have been released domestically per year in the last fifteen year. The bottom row (blue) presents releases by MPAA studios and their subsidiaries.[18] The top row (red) represents releases by non-MPAA members.

---

[16] Cp. MPAA (2009), p. 4, last accessed: 24.05.2015.
[17] Cp. MPAA (2015), p. 9, last accessed: 24.05.2015.
[18] Member studios include: Walt Disney Studios Motion Pictures, Paramount Pictures Corporation, Sony Pictures Entertainment, Twentieth Century Fox Film Corporation, Universal City Studios LLC and Warner Bros. Entertainment Inc., cp. MPAA (2015), p. 21, last accessed: 24.05.2015.

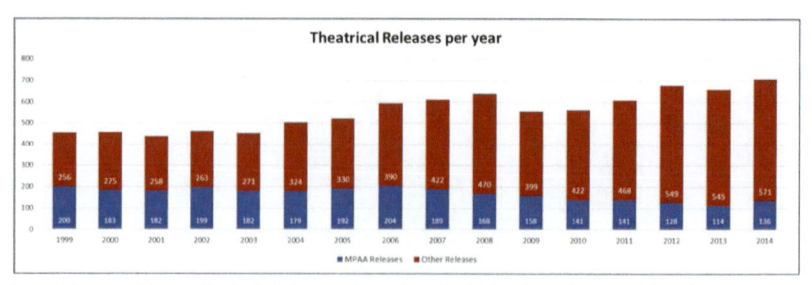

Fig.4: Number of Domestic Movie Releases, based on: MPAA (2015), p. 21; MPAA (2009), p. 5.

In 1999, the MPAA studios released 200 motion pictures (44% of all domestic movie releases), while non-MPAA members released 256 motion pictures (56% of all domestic movie releases).[19] This situation has changed dramatically in the last 15 years. While MPAA studio releases are down to 136 (19% of all domestic releases) releases in 2014, non-MPAA studios releases are up to 571, accounting for 81% of all domestic releases.[20]

As can be seen in Figure 4, films released by MPAA studios increased in 2014 for the first time in five years, up from 2013 by 19%. Total films released (up 7%) and films by Non-MPAA affiliated independents (up 5%) also increased from 2013.[21]

By using global industry data, this chapter provided an overview of the theatrical market. The key findings can be summed upped as follows:

- Box office revenues are growing faster in the rest of the world than domestically (in the United States and Canada).

- Foreign Box Revenues peaked in 2014, reaching a share of more than 70% of the global box office.

- The domestic box office has only grown slightly in the past fifteen years and declined in 2014 compared to the previous year.

- Domestic ticket sales are on a downwards trend as well with ticket price increases not being able to mitigate the lower sales numbers.

---

[19] Cp. MPAA (2009), p. 5, last accessed: 24.05.2015.
[20] Cp. MPAA (2015), p. 21, last accessed: 24.05.2015.
[21] Cp. MPAA (2015), p. 21, last accessed: 24.05.2015.

- Of the 707 motion pictures released in 2014 domestically, 571 were released by Non-MPAA independent affiliates.

- The share of Major studio motion picture releases of all domestic movie releases decreased from 44% in 1999 to 19% in 2014.

5.2.2   REVENUES FROM FOREIGN MARKETS

With the general theatrical market overview out of the way, the focus can now shift towards the first research questions. The objective is to attempt to quantify, how important revenues from foreign markets are for Hollywood Studios and how that importance has changed in the past fifteen years. The previous chapter already gave an overview of the general distribution of the global box office from a neutral perspective. In this chapter as well as Chapter 5.2.3, this thesis will take a different perspective: The analysis will be carried out from the point of view of an U.S. based studio. The data used in this chapter as well as Chapter 5.2.3 originates from various motion picture industry databases, which will be referenced accordingly.

Figure 5 illustrates the domestic and foreign box office revenues as a percentage of total box office revenues for the Top 100 domestic releases in each of the last fifteen years. The bottom row (blue) represents the percentage of domestic revenues and the top row (red) the percentage of foreign revenues.

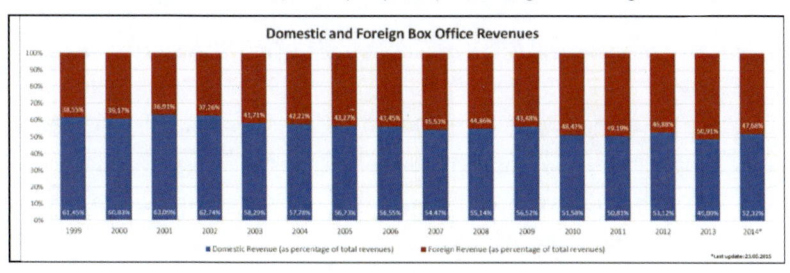

Fig.5: Distribution of Domestic and Foreign Box Office Revenues, based on: Information courtesy of Box Office Mojo (http://www.boxofficemojo.com).

In 1999, the Top 100 domestic motion pictures grossed 61.45% of their total revenue domestically, with the remaining 38.55% being contributed by foreign markets. In 2014, the Top 100 motion pictures still earned the majority of their revenues domestically (52.32%) with foreign markets contributing the remaining 47.68%. An increase in the share of more than 9% in the last fifteen years. Figure 5 shows a clear trend: The slow decline of the share in domestic box office revenues and the corresponding increase of the share of foreign revenues – and already once, in 2013, did the share of foreign box office revenues eclipse the share of domestic revenues.

In order to provide a better understanding of foreign box office revenues, Figure 6 shows in how many countries the widest release opened (blue bar on the left) and the average amount of countries the Top 100 motion pictures opened (red bar on the right).

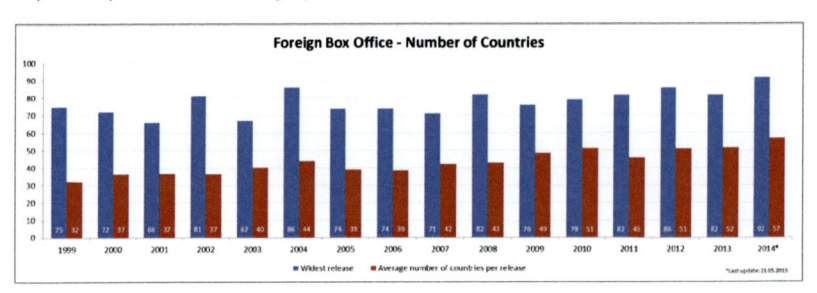

Fig.6: Foreign Releases, based on: Information courtesy of IMDb (http://www.imdb.com).

The results are somewhat surprising: 1999's *Star Wars: Episode I - The Phantom Menace* already opened in 75 different countries around the globe. That is the same amount of countries 2014's *Godzilla* opened in. These numbers suggest that it highly depends on the motion picture itself, rather than the available infrastructure: Blockbuster movies with mass appeal were able to open in dozens of different countries fifteen years ago, just as they are today. The widest released motion picture of 2014 was released in 92 countries, a moderate 22.6% increase, when compared to the widest release from 1999.

However, when looking at the average amount of countries the Top 100 motion pictures of a given year have been released in, a clear trend can be identified. While in 1999 the Top 100 movies were released in an average of 32 countries, they are released in 57 different countries in 2014, an increase of 78.1%. This suggests that especially mid-budget motion pictures have gained an increased exposure in recent years, being seen in 25 more countries - on average - than in 1999.

Now that the distribution of revenues as well as foreign releases have been examined more closely, the first research question can be answered:

- Revenues from the foreign box office play an important role for Hollywood studios. They currently account for around half of the total revenues.[22]

- The importance of foreign box office revenues has increased over the last fifteen years – while foreign box office revenues accounted for 40% of total revenues ten year ago, the share is up to around 50% in 2014.[23]

- When looking at the Top 100 motion pictures of each of the last fifteen years, the share of foreign box office revenues increased on average by only 0.6% per year or 9% in fifteen year. This represents a tremendous growth opportunity for Hollywood studios.[24]

- The importance of foreign box office revenues can be expected to continue to increase, this is fueled by a variety of factors:
    - Declining domestic attendance
    - Growth opportunities on foreign markets

---

[22] This is not a new observation. Vogel, who analyzed data from 1993-2009, confirms that "the top 100 films of any year have been consistent in drawing approximately half of their total box-office income in foreign markets", cf. Vogel (2011), p. 135.

[23] The increase can be explained by two different effects: (I) access to more countries as highlighted in Figure 6 and (II) more screens / better infrastructure per country. The latter effect was not explicitly discussed. However, the discussion in Chapter 5.2.1 highlighted that China became the first international market to exceed $4 billion in box office revenues, which is a good example for this effect.

[24] In contrast, the share of foreign box office revenues of the global box office grew by 21% in the same time frame as discussed in Chapter 5.2.1.

- Technical and/or infrastructure advancements allowing access to previously inaccessible territories (more countries and more markets per country)

5.2.3 Creativity in Hollywood

Now that the importance of foreign box office revenues has been discussed, the focus will shift towards the second research questions. The objective is to find out, if Hollywood studios have lost their creativity in an attempt to successfully serve as many international markets as possible.

The connection between foreign box office revenues and the discussion about creativity in Hollywood are related as was highlighted in Chapter 5.1. Some industry practitioners[25] as well as some media outlets[26] argue, that the dependence on foreign markets for profits, directly influences the type of motion pictures that are being made. They argue that Major studios are increasingly producing sequels and franchises, as it is easier to market motion pictures, which are either already established or have the potential to be established as a multi-movie franchise. Rather than going with an original idea, studios will rather use well-known properties and/or characters – be it a toy like "Battleship" or "G.I. Joe" or a series of novels like the "Hunger Games" series. Accordingly, creativity in the context of this paper is understood as the ability and willingness to produce original content.

By using the data of the Top 100 domestic motion picture releases per year, an attempt can be made to assess if Hollywood has indeed lost its' creativity and Studios are increasingly producing sequels and/or franchise movies based on established properties. Figure 7 shows the amount of sequels and franchise movies among the Top 100 domestic motion pictures for each of the last fifteen years.

---

[25] Cp. Obst, L. (2013), p. 36-41.
[26] Cp. Variety (2015), w/o p., last accessed 24.03.2015.

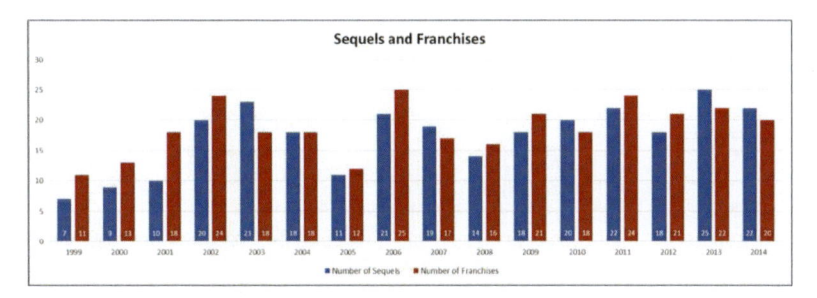

Fig.7: Sequel and Franchise Distribution, based on: Information courtesy of Box Office Mojo (http://www.boxofficemojo.com).

The left bar (blue) shows the amount of sequels and the right bar (red) show the amount of movies that a part of a franchise. The year 2006 saw the highest amount of movies that are part of a franchise, while 2013 had the most sequels, each accounting for one fourth of the 100 motion pictures examined in that particular year.

While a general trend towards more sequels and franchises seems to have occurred with the change of the millennium, there are also outliers like the years 2005 and 2008, where the amount of sequels and franchises is comparably low. A clear trend and a direct correlation with the importance of foreign box office revenues cannot be established: The share of foreign box office revenue grew in 2005 compared to 2004, while the amount of sequels and franchises dropped sharply in 2005 when compared to the previous year - to one of the lowest amounts in recent years.

It is also worth pointing out, that Hollywood has always produced sequels and franchises. In 1984, more than thirty years ago, the following seven motion pictures can all be found in the Top 10 for the year - each of them, either already part of a franchise or kicking off a franchise, which shaped the motion picture landscape in the years after 1984:

- Beverly Hills Cop
- Ghostbusters

- Indiana Jones and the Temple of Doom
- Gremlins
- The Karate Kid
- Police Academy
- Star Trek III: The Search for Spock

Now that the amount of sequels and franchises has been quantified, the focus will shift to another aspect - the idea sources for motion pictures. There are many different sources for an idea.[27] The following list includes some popular examples. Movies can be based on:

- Real life events (e.g. American Sniper)
- Fiction book or short story (e.g. Hunger Games)
- Comic or graphic novel (e.g. Guardians of the Galaxy)
- Toy (e.g. Lego Movie)
- Folk tale, legend or fairytale (e.g. Into the Woods)
- Original Screenplay (e.g. Big Hero 6)

An original screenplay is generally considered the most creative, as in this case, a writer or a group of writers creates everything from scratch, including but not limited to characters, the environment and story line.[28]

Figure 8 illustrates some of the popular sources for the Top 100 domestic motion picture release in each of the last fifteen years. The left bar (blue) represents the amount of movies based on original screenplays, the middle bar (red) the amount of movies based on a fiction book or short story and the bar on the right the number of movies based on a comic a graphic novel.

---

[27] For a better understanding about the different routes an idea can take towards a full screenplay commission cp. Wrobel, F. (2014), p. 78; Finney, A. (2010). pp. 23-24.
[28] Cp. Finney, A. (2010). p. 22-24.

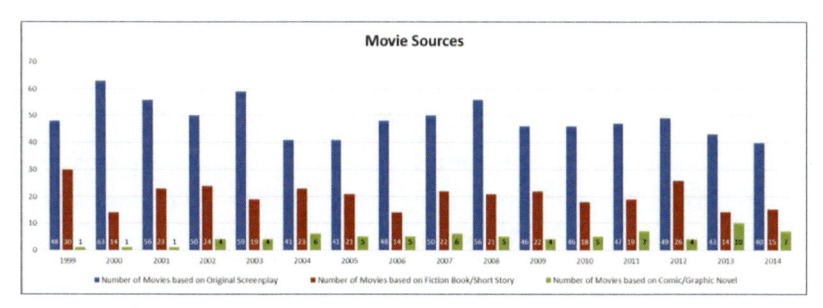

Fig.8: Movie Sources, based on: Information courtesy of Nash Information Services, LLC (http://www.the-numbers.com).

The number of movies based on an original screenplay peaked in 2000 with 63 of the Top 100 domestic motion pictures being based on an original screenplay. The same number fell to the lowest point of the last fifteen years in 2014 with only 40 motion pictures being based on an original screenplay. However, more than ten years ago, in 2004 and 2005, the number wasn't much higher with only one more motion picture being based on an original screenplay.

A clear trend, other than the increase in super hero movies based on comic book properties in recent years, cannot be identified. Their also seems to be no correlation between sequels/franchises and the sources motion pictures are based on.

In regards to the second research questions, the analysis of the Top 100 domestic releases in each of the least fifteen years revealed that there is no evidence that the importance of foreign box office revenues altered the product, the motion picture itself, in any significant way. As such there is no evidence that supports the claim that Hollywood has lost its' creativity.

5.3 Summary and Outlook

5.3.1 Summary

Motivated by claims of a "Broken Hollywood"[29], some of the changes that have occurred on the theatrical market in the past fifteen years have been examined in the previous chapter by using industry data as well as meta-data collected for 1500 movies of the past fifteen years.

The first research questions the analysis answered is, how important revenues from foreign markets are for Hollywood Studios and how the importance has changed in the past 15 years. The analysis revealed that:

- The importance of foreign box office revenues has indeed increased over the last 15 years, with foreign box office revenues currently accounting for roughly half of the total revenues.

- Foreign markets represent a tremendous growth opportunity for Hollywood studios. They grow faster than the domestic market and U.S. studios have not yet been able to increase their foreign share at a similar growth rate.

In order to be able to answer the second research questions and find out if Hollywood has indeed lost its' creativity and studios are increasingly producing sequels and/or franchise movies based on established properties, the distribution of sequels and franchises among the Top 100 motion pictures as well as the sources the movies are based on have also been examined.

The analysis produced no evidence that the importance of foreign box revenues altered the product in any significant way. The majority of movies produced in any given year are based on original screenplays, the exact amount fluctuated widely in the past fifteen years. The same can be said for sequels and franchises, the vast majority of movies are neither sequels nor part of a franchise. The actual amount of franchises or sequels in any given year varies widely and seems to be in no correlation with foreign box office growth.

---

[29] Cf. Variety (2015), w/o p., last accessed 24.03.2015.

Hollywood's Major Studios are certainly in a period of transition and changing economics, resulting in different strategies for the future. To claim however, that Hollywood is broken, as some industry practitioners do, seems to be exaggerated. The analysis conducted in this thesis allows the reader to put claims about foreign box office revenues, the lack of creativity and the general state of the industry in better perspective.

5.3.2 OUTLOOK

Digitalization impacts the motion picture industry in three distinct ways:[30]

1. Transaction cost are reduced for sellers
2. Search cost are reduced for buyers
3. The cost for producing and reproducing are reduced

This started a transformation process that incorporates all industry participants and is going on since at least 1999. While certain aspects of this transformation have been examined in detail, for example changing customer preferences and behavior[31], other aspects have not been given much attention at all, like intermediation. Consequently, contributions on related topics like changes in the value added structure[32], deliver questionable results.[33]

As mentioned in Chapter 5.1, this thesis is part of a larger research project – a dissertation, in which the changes that have occurred in the past fifteen years will be examined and explained in detail. The focus of the analysis will be on intermediation, as intermediaries play a vital part in the value system of the motion picture industry. To conduct the analysis, a new intermediation analysis approach will be developed and applied to the motion picture industry.

---

[30] Cp. Elberse, A. (2013), pp. 154-155.
[31] Cp. Mitomo, H., Otsuka, T. (2010), pp. 155-170.
[32] Cp. Eliashberg, J. et al. (2006), pp. 638–661; Hawkins, R., Vickery, G. (2008), pp. 60-63; Küng, L. (2008), pp. 71-73; Bloore, P. (2009), pp. 6-10; Finney, A. (2010), p. 11.
[33] For a comparison and evaluation of the various value added models of the motion picture industry introduced in recent years, cp. Wrobel, F. (2014), pp. 71-72.

The topics discussed in this thesis have a direct impact on the main body of work. The increasing importance of foreign revenues and the observation that movies are released in more and more countries suggests that the number of intermediaries in this particular part of the value system has increased.[34] The available literature on intermediation often suggests the contrary, namely that the number of intermediaries will decrease due to digitalization.[35]

The discussion about creativity in Hollywood is as much a discussion about strategy. Elberse formulated the *blockbuster strategy* or *winner-take-all* theory in 2013[36], which is a direct contradiction to Anderson's *long tail theory* formulated in 2005.[37] By using examples from various sectors of the entertainment industry, Elberse shows that the blockbuster movie with a risky high production and marketing budget, that has the mass appeal to be released everywhere around the globe, is actually good business and the preferable strategy.[38]

Many of the contributions on intermediation and the changing value added structure of the motion picture industry were created in the years 2006-2010, after the long tail theory was formulated. Some authors predict disintermediation to occur, especially in the independent sector of the motion picture industry. This prediction is partly based on the long tail theories' idea of finally being able to effectively serve niche audiences due to technological advancements, allowing direct contact between producers and end-consumer, thus eliminating intermediaries in between.[39]

Elberse uses the iTunes music store as an example of how such direct contact between artist and end-consumer ends up in practice: 102 songs (0.001%) of the eight million tracks sold in 2011 on iTunes sold more than one million units and accounted for 15% of total sales. The numbers at the end of tail are even more astonishing: 94% of all tracks sold fewer than 100 units and an incredible 32% of all tracks sold only one copy each.[40]

---

[34] This is because local distribution is usually handled by a local distributor. Additional sales agents are likely to be involved as well.
[35] Cp. Bloore, P. (2009), p. 17; Finney, A. (2010a), p. 17.
[36] Cp. Elberse, A. (2013), p. 163.
[37] Cp. Anderson, C. (2008), pp. 53-56.
[38] Cp. Elberse, A. (2013), p. 6.
[39] Cp. Bloore, P. (2009), p. 17; Finney, A. (2010a), p. 17.
[40] Cp. Elberse, A. (2013), pp. 159-161.

The data of the Top 100 motion pictures of the past fifteen years supports the success of a blockbuster strategy.[41] The head as well as the end of the tail will be examined in more detail in the dissertation. This analysis also has a direct impact on intermediation as a blockbuster strategy can only be executed with the help of intermediaries, e.g. agencies for social media and marketing as well as a distribution network, sales network, etc.

The dissertation project is scheduled to be completed in 2016 and published in 2017.

---

[41] With only very few exceptions, the movies with the highest production budgets consistently outperform their mid-budget peers in profitability.

REFERENCES

Monographs:

Anderson, C. (2008): The Longer Long Tail, 2nd ed., New York 2008.

Elberse, A. (2013): Blockbusters: Why Big Hits – and Big Risks – are the Future of the Entertainment Business, New York 2013.

Finney, A. (2010): The International Film Business: A Market Guide Beyond Hollywood, London 2010.

Hawkins, R., Vickery, G. (2008): Remaking the Movies: Digital Content and the Evolution of the Film and Video Industries, Paris 2008.

Küng, L. (2008): Strategic Management in the Media: Theory to Practice, London 2008.

Mitomo, H., Otsuka, T. (2010): Preference for Flat-Rate Media Access Fees: A Behavioural Economics Interpretation, in: Badillo, P.Y., Lesourd, J.B (eds.) (2010): The Media Industries and their Markets – Quantitative Analyses, New York 2010, pp. 155-170.

Obst, L. (2013): Sleepless in Hollywood – Tales from the New Abnormal in the Movie Business, New York 2013.

Vogel, H.L. (2011): Entertainment Industry Economics – A Guide for Financial Analysis, 8th ed., New York 2011.

Wrobel, F. (2014): Digital Video and Disintermediation in the Value System of the Motion Picture Industry, Aachen 2014.

Journals and Essays:

Bloore, P. (2009): Re-defining the Independent Film Value Chain, Norwich 2009, available online: http://industry.bfi.org.uk/media/pdf/h/b/Film_Value_Chain_Paper.pdf, last accessed: 20.03.2015.

Eliashberg, J., Elberse, A., Leenders, M.A.A.M. (2006): The Motion Picture Industry: Critical Issues in Practice, Current Research, and New Research Directions, in Marketing Science, Vol. 25, No. 6, pp. 638–661.

Finney, A. (2010a): Value Chain Restructuring in the Global Film Industry, Grenoble 2010, available online: http://ec.europa.eu/culture/ media/programme/docs/public_cons_media2010/44.pdf, last accessed: 20.03.2015.

Internet Sources:

Box Office Mojo (2015): Yearly Grosses, available on: http://www.boxofficemojo.com/yearly/, last accessed: 23.05.2015.

IMDb (2015): Country Release Data, available on: http://www.imdb.com, last accessed: 23.05.2015.

Nash Information Services (2015): Movie Idea Sources, available on: http://www.the-numbers.com, last accessed: 23.05.2015.

MPA (2006) MPA Market Statistic 2005, available on: http://www.stop-runaway-production.com/wp-content/uploads/2009/07/2005-MPAA-Market-Stats-26-pages.pdf, last accessed: 24.05.2015.

MPA (2005) MPA Market Statistic 2004, available on: http://www.immagic.com/eLibrary/ARCHIVES/GENERAL/MPAA_US/M050309M.pdf, last accessed: 24.05.2015.

MPA (2003) MPA Market Statistic 2002, available on: http://www.stop-runaway-production.com/wp-content/uploads/2009/07/2002-MPAA-Market-Stats-60-pages.pdf, last accessed: 24.05.2015.

MPAA (2015): Theatrical Market Statistics 2014, available on: http://www.mpaa.org/wp-content/uploads/2015/03/MPAA-Theatrical-Market-Statistics-2014.pdf, last accessed: 24.05.2015.

MPAA (2014): Theatrical Market Statistics 2013, available on: http://www.mpaa.org/wp-content/uploads/2014/03/MPAA-Theatrical-Market-Statistics-2013_032514-v2.pdf, last accessed: 24.05.2015.

MPAA (2013): Theatrical Market Statistics 2012, available on: http://www.mpaa.org/wp-content/uploads/2014/03/2012-Theatrical-Market-Statistics-Report.pdf, last accessed: 24.05.2015.

MPAA (2012): Theatrical Market Statistics 2011, available on: http://www.bumpercarfilms.com/assets/downloads/movies.pdf, last accessed: 24.05.2015.

MPAA (2011): Theatrical Market Statistics 2010, available on: http://www.stop-runaway-production.com/wp-content/uploads/2009/07/2010-MPAA-market-stats.pdf, last accessed: 24.05.2015.

MPAA (2010): Theatrical Market Statistics 2009, available on: http://www.womeninfilm.ca/_Library/docs/MPAATheatricalMarketStatistics2009.pdf, last accessed: 24.05.2015.

MPAA (2009): Theatrical Market Statistics 2008, available on: http://www.stop-runaway-production.com/wp-content/uploads/2009/07/2008-MPAA-Theatrical-Stats.pdf, last accessed: 24.05.2015.

MPAA (2008): Entertainment Industry Market Statistics 2007, available on: https://robertoigarza.files.wordpress.com/2008/11/rep-entertainment-industry-market-statistics-mp-2007.pdf, last accessed: 24.05.2015.

THR (2013): Steven Spielberg Predicts 'Implosion' of Film Industry, available on: http://www.hollywoodreporter.com/news/steven-spielberg-predicts-implosion-film-567604, last accessed: 24.03.2015.

Variety (2015): Broken Hollywood: The Biz's Top Players Call Out Ways Industry Needs to Change, available on: http://variety.com/2015/film/news/broken-hollywood-the-bizs-top-players-call-out-ways-industry-needs-to-change-1201416866/, last accessed: 24.03.2015.

The Authors

Chul-Young Byun

In 2000 Chul-Young Byun started his professional career as an IT project manager after having completed his business mathematician degree at the Technical University in Berlin, Germany.

Today, Chul-Young Byun works in the area of strategic IT management for a multinational clinical research organization. Besides his daily job he lectures on project management at private universities and works on his PhD thesis with the focus on IT project risk management.

Chul-Young Byun lives with his wife and daughters in Berlin, Germany.

Katrin Kanzenbach

Diploma in teaching (TU Dresden), Master's degree in Law, LL.M. and Management (Human Resources), M.A. at FOM University of Applied Sciences in Nuremberg and Stuttgart, Experience of working in HR development at Allianz AG, Head of personnel development, Working experience as Commercial Lawyer in a small-sized company, Academic working experience at Universities, Recent teaching experience at higher education at FHAM Erding.

Tobias Lippe

My name is Tobias Lippe and I was born in September, 1984. I achieved my Bachelor in International Business and Management at Fontys in Venlo, Netherlands and continued with my Master at the University of Plymouth, Great Britain in 2010. Afterwards I started my career in Frankfurt/Main as a managerial accountant, where I worked till 2012. From 2012-2014 I returned to Fontys in Venlo and worked as a lecturer for Finance. In 2014 I started my current job as a managerial accountant / analyst in Gelsenkirchen.

Agnieszka Michniuk

For nearly five years Agnes Michniuk is working at the Software company Hanse Orga AG in Hamburg. She started as a Consultant in the area of SAP Finance and for two years she is working as a Project Manager. Currently she is sharing the leadership of a Payment Factory project at Deutsche Lufthansa AG with a colleague and is leading a Cash and Liquidity Management Projekt at SWISS International Airlines in Switzerland. Before she joined Hanse Orga AG she did her Master of Science in Management Studies at the University of Flensburg and worked as a student trainee at the IT subsidiary of the municipal utility Flensburg, IT Power, in the area of SAP project- and resource planning. Her specialisation during the Master degree was Finance, Entrepreneurship and Management Consulting.

Prior to that, she finished her Bachelor of Science in International Management at the University of Flensburg. During her Bachelor studies she spent one year abroad at the California State University of Sacramento (CSUS) in Sacramento, USA. At the CSUS she was enrolled in the Business Administration department and took courses in Finance, Operation Management and Marketing (Buyer Behavior).

Florian Wrobel

Florian has several years of experience in IT Security and IT Project Management in various industry sectors. He is currently a Senior Consultant for Information Security based in Munich, Germany. His focus areas are the implementation of Information Security Management Systems (ISMS), the conduction of vulnerability analyses and risk assessment as well as the implementation of data privacy requirements. Florian completed his Bachelor degree in Business Administration in 2007 and his Master degree in Business Administration in 2012. His research is focused on the impact of digitalization on industry structures, particularly on the structure of the various sectors of the media industry.

Chul-Young Byun
Software Development Project Risk Management – Enhancement of Existing Theories
Supervisors:
Prof. Dr. Mercedes Carmona
Prof. Dr. Thomas Heupel

Katrin Kanzenbach
The Role of the Compliance Officer – a Comparison of U.S., U.K. and German Law and Practice
Supervisors:
Prof. Dr. Diego Manzanares
Prof. Dr. Olaf Müller-Michaels

Tobias Lippe
Critical analysis of the precision of valuations in financial experts' fairness opinions
Supervisor:
Prof. Dr. Juan Cándido
Prof. Dr. Stefan Heinemann

Agnieszka Michniuk
Social comparison as a mediator variable between communication design and purchase intention
Supervisors:
Prof. Dr. Conchi Parra
Prof. Dr. Oliver Gansser

Florian Wrobel
Digitalization and Motion Pictures: A Theatrical Market Analysis
Supervisors:
Prof. Dr. Mercedes Carmona
Prof. Dr. Peter Kürble

FOLGENDE BÄNDE SIND BISHER IN DIESER REIHE ERSCHIENEN

Band 1 (2015)
Yearbook 2014
978-3-8440-3445-5

Band 2 (2015)
Yearbook 2015
978-3-8440-4040-1